EPHEMERA OF TRAVEL & TRANSPORT

EPHEMERA
of
TRAVEL
and
TRANSPORT

Janice Anderson
and Edmund Swinglehurst

With an introduction by Maurice Rickards,
Founder of The Ephemera Society

New Cavendish Books

Companion volume 'Street Jewellery'
by Christopher Baglee & Andrew Morley
ISBN 0 904568 16 4

First edition published in Great Britain
by New Cavendish Books—1981

Design—John B. Cooper
Editorial and production—A & N Levy
Printed and bound in England by Waterlow (Dunstable) Ltd.
Colour separation by WT Graphics, London

New Cavendish Books
11 New Fetter Lane, London EC4P 4EE
Distribution: ABP, North Way, Andover, Hampshire SP10 5BE

ISBN 0 904568 27 X

CONTENTS

ACKNOWLEDGEMENTS

The authors and publisher extend their thanks to the following members of the Ephemera Society, from whose collections the selection of items reproduced here was drawn.

Dr. J. A. Ambrose
Jane Babson
H. Beresford-Bourke
Beamish Open Air Museum
Sarah de Beaumont
Drene Brennan
Henry Bristow
John Buist
Iain Campbell
Thomas Cook Group Ltd
Andrew Cunningham
Dunlop Ltd
Barrie Evans
Elizabeth Farrow
Valerie and Stanley
   Friedman
Elizabeth Greig
Barbara Grigor-Taylor
Guildhall Library
George Jasieniecki
John Hall
Valerie Harris
Frances Henshaw
Graham Hudson
Rank Hovis Ltd
William Itoh
Imperial War Museum
Peter Jackson
Frances Keefe
Yvonne Knight

Dave L'Affineur
Stephen Lash
Allen Levy
Museum of London
Brian Love
Michael Lyne
John Martin
Jocelyn P. Mullinger
Calvin P. Otto
Graham Page
James Packer
Jim Parkinson
Richard Perfitt
Maurice Rickards
J. Sainsbury Ltd.
Amoret Scott
Laura Seddon
Ken and Iliassa Sequin
Julie Skjold
Richard Storey
J. A. B. Taylor
Frank Teagle
Brigadier C. R. Templer
Denis Vandervelde
John Vaughan
John Walker & Sons Ltd.
Malkolm Warrington
Derek White
Jeanette White
Bill Wright

Thanks are also due to the Council of the Ephemera Society for their kind cooperation, and particularly to Elizabeth Greig, who devised and organised the exhibition 'Going Places' in which the ephemera featured here originally appeared, and through whose initiative this publication was conceived.

THE EPHEMERA SOCIETY

Patron   Lord Asa Briggs
President Sir John Betjeman
Council   Maurice Rickards, FSIAD FIIP *Chairman*
            Calvin P. Otto *Chairman North American Office*
            Patrick Hickman Robertson *Secretary*
            John Hall ARCA NDD *Treasurer*
            Anthony Ambrose BSc MA PhD
            Sarah du Boscq de Beaumont BA
            Elizabeth Greig BA MCSP
            Graham Hudson MSIAD NDD ATD
            Peter Jackson
            Brian Love ARCA NDD
            Amoret Scott

The Ephemera Society is concerned with the preservation, study and educational uses of printed and handwritten ephemera—the minor documents of everyday life.

The term 'ephemera' covers a wide range of marginalia from tickets to letterheads, from labels to proclamations. Collectors of ephemera vary in their approach. Some are interested in social-history content; some view specimens as items of printing history; others collect them simply as evocative reminders of the past. Yet others collect ephemera of today, the trivia that will become the social-history and typographic bygones of tomorrow.

The full range of collectors' items is vast. It includes such widely varying items as leaflets, notices, receipts, trade cards, laundry lists, certificates, summonses, bills of lading, licences, indentures, permits, rent demands, timetables, tax forms, wrappers, magazines, newspapers, sale notices, membership cards, menus, notices-to-quit, mourning cards, instruction sheets, handbills, greeting cards, school reports, advertising novelties, posters—the full spectrum of everyday life expressed in marginalia.

For the most part these are inexpensive items, often neglected oddments rescued from attic or paper-bin. Their value lies solely in their appeal to the eye of the rescuer.

There are also more costly pieces, items whose age, content or rarity confers on them a particular significance. These are the 'specials' of ephemera collecting, the early nineteenth-century transportation orders, the press-gang permits and the schooner bills of lading.

In general, the collector enjoys an undemanding level of expense. Unlike his counterpart in other fields, the ephemerist may buy modestly. Indeed, for the specialist who favours items of today's ephemera, the majority of specimens are free of all charge.

As well as being collected for their own sake, items of ephemera provide a graphic background to history. From salvaged trade cards, leaflets, advertising material and sale and auction notices the historian may reconstruct a picture of a vanished age. Whole neighbourhoods, or even a single street, may live again in a collection of printed and written fragments. The development of trades and industries, national, regional or local, may be traced in the same way.

The Ephemera Society exists not only to further the interests of the collector but to encourage interest in ephemera among a wider public. It sees that the conservation of ephemera relies as much on an informed public opinion as on the efforts of individual specialists. The Society invites everybody's cooperation and interest.

The Society forms a link between collectors, offering a means of contact, information and mutual assistance. Study meetings, lectures and visits are organised and there are numerous sales and exchange sessions. The Society also offers guidance on all matters of ephemera, including dating, storage, filing, conservation and possible sources (commercial or otherwise).

A further function of the Society is to serve as a formal clearing-house and repository for items of ephemera which might otherwise be destroyed. A number of collections have been deposited with the Society for this purpose. Government departments, commercial concerns and private individuals are invited to make use of this service.

A non-profit body founded in 1975, the Society quickly gained recognition as the authority in its field and as a source of information and advice on ephemera. It now counts among its members libraries, schools, colleges and universities and a number of museums as well as private individuals in half a dozen countries.

The Society's journal *The Ephemerist* carries news, articles and sales-and-wants announcements and is published quarterly to members. Exhibitions, TV, radio and press mentions bring increasing awareness of the archival value of ephemera to the public at large.

The Society's long-term plans include the setting up of a permanent archive and the initiating of research and educational projects.

Applications for membership are invited from any person interested in the conservation and study of printed or handwritten ephemera, whether as private collector, institutional archivist or antiquarian.

The Society's address is:
12 Fitzroy Square, London W1P 5HQ

North America:
Calvin P. Otto, 124 Elm Street,
Bennington, Vermont 05201, USA

Collecting Ephemera

by Maurice Rickards

The term 'ephemera' is broadly defined by members of the Ephemera Society as 'the minor transient documents of everyday life'. It covers an immense field. It includes the many thousands of printed and handwritten oddments that civilisation pours out every day—tickets, labels, leaflets, receipts, wrappers, menus, stationery—the whole spectrum of everyday living expressed in scraps of paper.

The list is endless. There is hardly a single aspect of human affairs that does not yield its quota of printed or handwritten record. Greeting cards, school reports, certificates and permits, advertising novelties, bills of lading, summonses, tax forms, letterheads, rent demands, magazines and newspapers, membership cards, laundry lists—all of these are mementoes of the occasions that produce them.

Often, in spite of the diligence and efficiency of the formal historian, these fragments represent our only evidential link. Most of them are printed and produced for the very briefest of useful lives—though some, we may observe, have greater expectations. The bus ticket may flourish for a few minutes; the marriage licence appreciably longer! On the whole, as their name indicates (*ephemeral*: lasting for a day), they are as transient as the mayfly.

In recent years, the study and conservation of ephemera has attracted increasing attention. The power of these fragments, not only to record the factual detail of the moment but to evoke and express its spirit, has struck an ever widening public. The 'academic' student of ephemera, the social historian, the graphic designer and printing-history specialist, have been joined by the informed layman and the general collector. With the founding of the Ephemera Society in London in 1975, the interests of these various groups were brought together in a single organisation. The Society's fifth annual exhibition, featuring items from the collections of over sixty of its members, took for its theme the subject of travel and transport. Under the title 'Going Places', the exhibition provided a kaleidoscopic view of the whole history of man's restlessness—paper fragments from the age of the stage coach to space exploration—and this book, compiled and produced with the help of the Ephemera Society, presents the essence of a show which later was to tour the country as the Society's contribution to World Ephemera Year, 1980.

Few subjects have such universal appeal as travel and transport. Few are expressed as graphically and comprehensively through the medium of ephemera. The travel ticket, at once the most commonplace and most evocative of mementoes, is just one of a multitude of travellers' collectibles. To the list of ordinary 'booking office' souvenirs we may add a colourful parade of second-line stuff—baggage labels, resort stickers, travel folders, posters and handbills, ship-board menus, passenger lists, airline boarding cards, stagecoach tickets, hotel brochures, touring maps, postcards, passports, timetables, broadsides—not to mention a raft or two of travel-orientated toys and games, music covers, confectionery wrappers, cigar labels, etc, etc.

Certainly there are few travellers—avowed collectors or not—whose private files do not disclose a memento of some unforgotten trip, a dog-eared ferryboat ticket, a long-lamented customs receipt, a rate-card from an hotel in Boulogne in 1957. . . Even for the non-collector there is a special appeal in ephemera, a certain nostalgic magic, which makes incipient collectors of us all.

The items illustrated in this book have been brought together by collectors of many kinds—housewives, businessmen, schoolchildren, museums, libraries, commercial

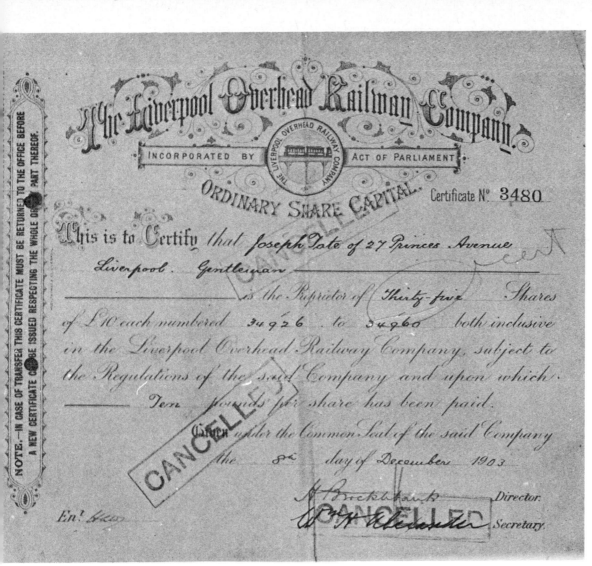

Early railway timetables were printed on cards. This clearly printed example is
from the earliest line of all—the Stockton and Darlington.
114 × 150mm

A risqué postcard with a double meaning suggesting a possible
romantic aspect to rail travel.
137 × 86mm

firms. Common to all has been a desire to conserve a fragment of the all-too-transient travel scene, a reminder, personal or general, of the adventure of progression from A to B.

Some collections are built around a theme; others around a specific category. Thus, within the overall theme of travel and transport, one collector may focus on a specialised area—'The Stagecoach Era', for example, or 'The Great Atlantic Liners' or 'Early Passenger Flights'. Here the objective is an 'ephemera picture' of the subject in all its aspects, using a miscellany of tickets, timetables, labels, advertising and other items to fill out the overall view.

For the 'category' collector, the focus is on ephemera of a given function. Here, still within the topic of travel and transport, we may find a specialised collection of passports, perhaps—or railway tickets, or bills of lading or carriers' trade cards or touring maps, or any one of a hundred special categories of ephemera. (Many collectors have it both ways: they may collect in certain areas by theme, in others by category.)

'Theme' collections sometimes develop as a result of one or two casual acquisitions, but for the most part they are expressions of the collector's pre-existing interests. The stagecoach enthusiast acquires stagecoach material as surely as railway items find their way to the railway collector and as motorists unerringly attract the ephemera of the wheel. (We observe, however, that not all ephemerists espouse the ephemera of their own occupation. A celebrated crime writer collects items related to the zeppelin; a lady lecturer in anatomy collects early cycling items; a well-known publisher collects the ephemera of model railways. . .)

Travel and transport themes may be as broad or as narrow as the individual cares. Many collectors settle for generalised topics—'Horse Power'; 'Ballooning'; 'The Paddle Steamer' etc. Others may restrict themselves to narrower fields: 'The History of the London Taxicab'; 'Early Railway Catering'; 'The Electric Road Vehicle'; 'Emigration'; 'The Development of Travel Health Controls'; 'Canal-Building in the Nineteenth Century'.

Travel and transport ephemera, as we have seen, may be collected by category. An individual collection may thus illustrate the evolution of a given form of document—the waybill, for transportation in every form; passports, passes and similar papers; timetables of all descriptions, and other such specific kinds of ephemera. A number of collectors confine themselves to railway tickets, others to platform tickets, others to luggage tickets. Tram and bus tickets are also the subjects of special collections; so are employee passes, season tickets and toll- and turnpike-tickets.

It must be said that however unpromising a given field may at first appear to the outsider, the majority of these specialised collections prove to be of absorbing interest—not only to their custodians but to the average friendly eye. Given the conscientious curatorship and background research that all collections demand, the most unlikely subject matter springs to life.

It is in its capacity for providing the ordinary citizen with opportunities of expertise that the collecting of ephemera offers its most engaging welcome. (Who can deny the pleasure of the distinction of being the world's first—and possibly sole—expert in the matter of, say, waggon-shunting labels, or ocean-liner baggage tags?) We may venture a smile, but we must seriously concede that here are fields unlimited—areas of a collector's individual choice—for original and perhaps significant research.

It is not without some satisfaction that the custodian and student of ephemera finds himself consulted on matters in his field, matters of historical detail for publishers and educationalists, authentic specimens for film and television companies, illustrations for social-history studies. The ephemerist is rarely just a hobbyist; however slight, however extensive, the collection is a form of archive, a work of reference and record.

Among its many attractions, not least is the ease with which the ephemera collector may make a start. Within a chosen field, theme or category, an almost immediate launch may be made with items of the present day. Many of these (in the present case, travel tags, labels, advertising handbills, etc.) are available more or less free of charge at any rail or coach station, port, or airport. With due discrimination, relevant material may be sifted from the general mass—items specifically culled to convey the collector's objective—and the shaping of the collection is under way. If, as often is the case, the collector seeks to illustrate historical development, now begins the fascinating task of moving backwards into time.

Yesterday's ephemera—items that illustrate the earlier stages of today's development—are to be found in a wide variety of places, some of them predictable, some wholly unexpected. Obvious sources are junk shops, market stalls, jumble sales, antiques and bygones fairs, antiquarian bookshops and auctions. Here the collector will

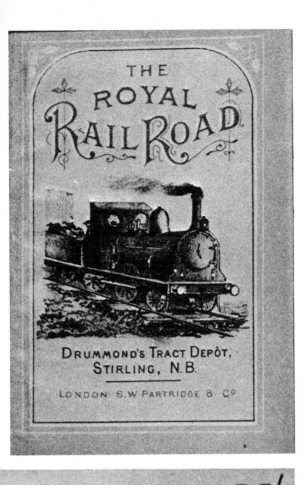

The handsomely-designed cover of a Scottish 'railway' religious tract.
115 × 79 mm

The Great Western and Michigan Railway issued this card featuring an interesting point on its route.
77 × 114 mm

Free passes, such as this French example, have always been recognised workers' 'perks' on the railway.
74 × 113 mm

Business card of the Hotel Schweizerhof at Interlaken. Opened in 1856, it was one of the first great Swiss hotels.
78 × 105 mm

Privilege tickets, such as this one for use between Crystal Palace and Ludgate Hill station in London, were often given to railway managers and important railway customers.
140 × 90 mm

Hotel suitcase labels, such as this one from a Quebec Hotel, were once the mark of the well-travelled man.
75 × 110mm

Ornately decorated menu card from the station buffet at Brunig in the Bernese Oberland.
125 × 85 mm

Just a very simple card, but this Venetian gondolier's business card could help recall many happy holiday memories.
69 × 115 mm

The travel agent, Thomas Cook, had a monopoly of Nile holiday steamer traffic before World War I. His steamers, such as the *MS Hatasoo* on this souvenir card, were built in Britain and assembled in Egypt.
70 × 146 mm

pay for his finds, much or little, according to the mood and calibre of the vendor, the nature of his overheads and his knowledge of the field. Built into the price will be not only the 'value' of the item (who can say, by the way, how much a long-expired season ticket or a 1920s waybill is worth?) but the convenience of the vendor's having rescued it and kept it for an indefinite period for the next purchaser.

Less financially demanding (and far less convenient) are the neglected attic, the forgotten trunk in the cellar, the rubbish dump, and even the waste-merchant's paper mountain. For the adventurous ephemerist, these represent the true source areas, the virgin goldfields of discovery. Also worth a second glance are premises where long-established businesses announce their coming removal—or renovation, or change of ownership, or final closure. In the upheaval of change, the paperwork of the past may prove too great a burden for those in charge of it, and by neglect or intention it vanishes for ever on a backyard bonfire. The ephemerist's timely intervention has rescued many hundreds of significant items—among them a number of those illustrated in this book.

As with the ephemera dealer, the exertions of the collector in his work of search and rescue must be taken into account in assessing monetary values. It is clear that neither lives in an economic vacuum, and both parties must remain solvent if they are to survive. It therefore appears right and proper that enterprise and exertion should receive reward; values emerge not by arbitrary nomination, but by the interplay of the classic economic forces of supply and demand, and any attempt to formalise price structure must fail.

It must be remembered too that scarcity value, a basic component of the market in most collecting fields, is here of only doubtful relevance. Printed ephemera, by definition the product of a mass process, offers few, if any, identifiably 'unique' items. Each specimen must stand or fall by the valuation the individual personally places on it, and today's 'catalogued' item may be available tomorrow from another source at much less than half the price.

Valuation of ephemera must remain for many years to come a matter of individual response. Though prices of ephemera (like those of newspapers and chocolates) may rise, the ephemerist must value his collection for its personal pleasure-content rather than primarily as an investment.

To the newcomer who asks 'What should I collect?' the answer is as simple and direct as it would be to the question 'What should I wear?' or 'What should I read?' The answer is 'Whatever you *like*'. Collecting that is undertaken as a business sideshow, or as a conceit, or in fulfilment of an imagined social compulsion is hollow. What shines from the true ephemerist's eye, whether his subject is travel and transport or eighteenth-century lottery tickets, is the excitement of the subject itself. If, over the years, the ephemera of his subject should incidentally increase in monetary value, that is a bonus to be grateful for, but not to count on.

Regardless of market values, the ephemerist's collection needs careful keeping. If it is to be studied and consulted, if it is to serve its purpose as a work of record, it must offer not only secure storage but easy access. Conservation, filing and display are the three basic imperatives in any collection that is anything more than a mere accumulation.

It is unfortunately true that, broadly speaking, the interests of conservation and display are incompatible. Whatever makes for easy access and examination tends to make for damage to the specimen; whatever guards the specimen from harm tends also to guard it from human scrutiny. The predicament has faced the professional curator since museums and libraries began. It faces the ephemerist (private and institutional) today. There is no easy answer. The collector of ephemera must compromise.

It must be continually borne in mind that items of ephemera are vulnerable from a number of quarters: acidification and embrittlement; fading and discoloration; attack by fungus of various kinds—and physical damage by handling.

By far the most common of these is damage by handling. It is not an overstatement to say that the most serious threat to the ephemerist's collection is presented by its owner. With each successive handling, specimens are imperceptibly—sometimes perceptibly—reduced in condition. Creasing, dog-ears, tattered edges, finger marks (visible and latent), all insidiously increase; minor abrasions and surface markings appear; fold fractures progressively weaken.

Not only the owner, but friends and fellow collectors who also leaf through the material contribute their portion to its destruction. The greater the 'use' made of it, in fact, the shorter its expectation of life. The solution, in principle, is to reduce movement and physical contact to a minimum.

An interim measure is the insertion of items in

transparent envelopes of the 'shirt bag' variety. These, having a polythene front for visibility and a paper back for response to variation in temperature and humidity, offer much protection. Their major disadvantages are twofold: they obscure the backs of double-sided items, and their long-term acidification properties are suspect. They do however greatly reduce the wear-and-tear effect of handling, and their use in transit and temporary storage is now more or less universal.

Permanent storage and display require the use of specifically non-acidic materials and a complete rejection of any method of mounting involving direct application of glues, gums or other fixative. This means very careful selection of mounts, albums or display folders, using slip-in retaining strips where these are practicable or transparent photo-corners to hold specimens in fixed positions.

It must be stressed that the matter of mounts, albums and display devices remains a vexed one. Only those specifically described by the manufacturer as acid-free are to be recommended, and only those plastic sheets guaranteed to be chemically inert should be used. Many of the plastic wallet-type album pages commonly available have been found to acquire the imprinted image of their content by chemical transfer, and the 'tacky page' album, in which the specimen adheres to the surface beneath a plastic sheet, should of course be rigorously avoided.

The problem of acid damage (recognised by its attendant effects of embrittlement and discoloration) is dealt with on a preventive basis by acid-free storage and display and, remedially, by deacidification. For the general collector this normally means the use of sachets or interleaves of calcium carbonate. (These, it must be borne in mind, have the effect of halting the progress of the trouble rather than reversing it.)

Fungoidal attack, normally appearing only in conditions of damp and enclosure, is treated in the first instance by drying out in freely circulating air and by fumigation with thymol.

Fading, brought about by exposure to light, is minimised by storage in the dark and display under Melinex, or similar transparent sheeting providing filtration of ultra-violet light.

In all of the more specialised aspects of care and conservation the serious collector will seek professional advice, but broadly speaking we may observe the following storage and display criteria: the system should be one in which specimens are presented, firmly (yet removable), in a non-injurious setting, without use of direct fixative and in such a way as to allow easy re-location as the collection develops. Ready access and visibility, with minimal wear-and-tear contact, are also major requirements.

Filing methods are matters for individual arrangement. Certainly no collection can survive as a going concern without one; certainly no filing system can meet the needs of every collection. As with many other aspects of ephemera collecting, individual enterprise and innovation will explore the way.

Cleaning and 'restoration' of ephemera should, on the whole, be avoided. One consideration is the undeniable right of elderly specimens to look their age. (What more disconcerting than a centuries-old document that looks as though it had been produced yesterday?) A further consideration is that as with people—most methods of 'rejuvenation' are in the long run deleterious.

Items of ephemera may be washed, bleached, ironed, trimmed and generally tinkered with, but it must be realised that each one of these tampering processes removes the specimen one stage further from the innocent veracity of its natural condition. Ephemera must be viewed as direct and untrammeled evidence—items as valuable in social-history research as papers in evidence in a court of law. What is needed is the evidence as it actually is, not as a concocted reconstruction. Tinkering, as well as serving to pervert the evidence, also subjects ephemera to processes it was never intended to suffer. As with hospital surgery, the experience is not to be undertaken lightly, nor indeed without pressing need.

It is a maxim among professional document-repair practitioners that no item may be submitted to a process which is not reversible. In other words, no repair must be carried out which does not allow the item, should it be desired, to be safely restored to its former 'unrepaired' state. The principle is a sound one. The ephemerist must remember that, once washed, ephemera cannot be unwashed. Nor can it be unbleached, untrimmed or unironed. Apart from the direst of emergencies, it is best left as it is.

Though some of its more specialised conservational aspects may appear daunting, there can be no doubt that the study of ephemera is among the least burdensome and most engaging of collecting interests. It is an activity well within the capability and financial scope of the ordinary citizen and an area in which, unlike most other collecting fields, a significant collection may be built at modest—even negligible—cost.

This book presents that proposition in action.

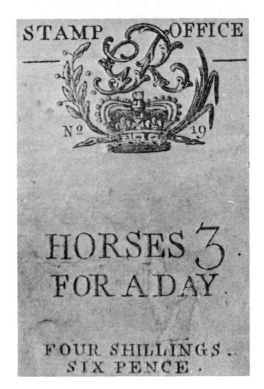

An elegant design for an everyday object: a Stamp Office receipt
for tax paid on hire of post horses.
94 × 62 mm

An ornate Edwardian trade card from a Cornish posting stable.
75 × 114 mm

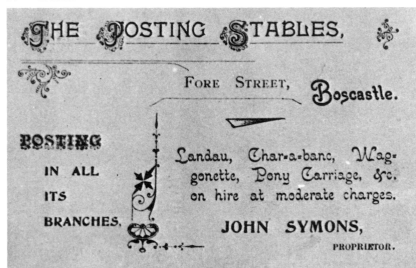

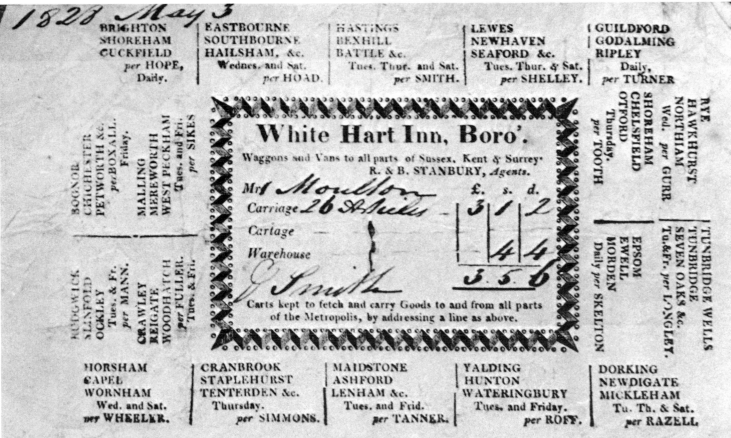

This London waggoner's bill shows an attractive freedom from
conventional styles, with its lists of destinations printed all round
the centre panel, but it is certainly effective.
114 × 167 mm

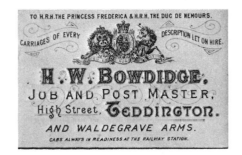

This 'post master's' trade card is also ornately designed, but is
much more stylish. The royal coat of arms helps, of course.
60 × 92 mm

Car pass for a private road, 1979.   63 × 120 mm

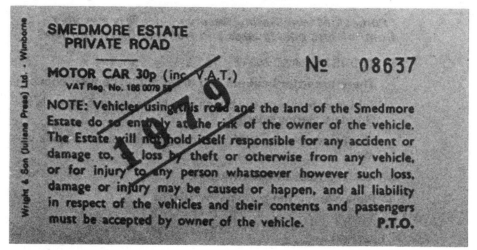

SMEDMORE ESTATE
PRIVATE ROAD
—
MOTOR CAR 30p (inc V.A.T.)
VAT Reg. No. 186 0079 59

No   08637

NOTE: Vehicles using this road and the land of the Smedmore
Estate do so entirely at the risk of the owner of the vehicle.
The Estate will not hold itself responsible for any accident or
damage to, or loss by theft or otherwise from any vehicle,
or for injury to any person whatsoever however such loss,
damage or injury may be caused or happen, and all liability
in respect of the vehicles and their contents and passengers
must be accepted by owner of the vehicle.   P.T.O.

Wright & Son (Juliana Press) Ltd. - Wimborne

Cigarette packets have become much sought-after by collectors.
This attractive example comes from a leading British
manufacturer.   73 × 66 mm

Radio taxi business card from London, 1970s.
67 × 104 mm

BE
SAFE
BE
SURE

USE
A
LICENSED
TAXI

RING
286 4848

Car park ticket from National Car Parks, a London company
which has profited from helping motorists park in the overcrowded
city.   93 × 91 mm

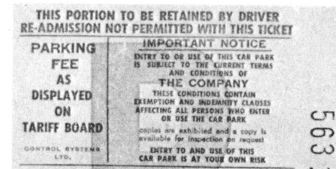

AUTO RENTING SERVICE
ANY TIME - ANY PLACE
WEDDINGS, FUNERALS AND CHRISTNENINGS.
LONG DISTANT TOURS A SPECIALTY
7 PASSENGER LIMOUSINE REASONABLE RATES
231 STATE STREET   R. J. TASH Prop.

PHONE 1188-J

American car hirer's business card.
66 × 96 mm

Another form of car park
ticket, this time a
coin-in-the-slot type from
the royal town of Windsor.
63 × 29 mm

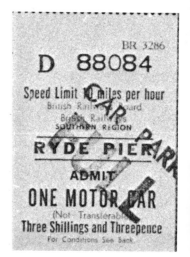

Ticket admitting one car on to
Ryde Pier, Isle of Wight, 1968.
62 × 43 mm

16

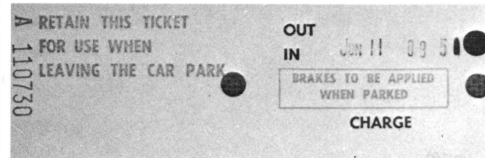

Alum Bay on the Isle of Wight is a popular spot with visitors, so the nearby Needles Hotel provides a useful car park. Ticket dating from 1968.
76 × 74 mm

Another style of windscreen sticker parking ticket, 1979.
44 × 127 mm

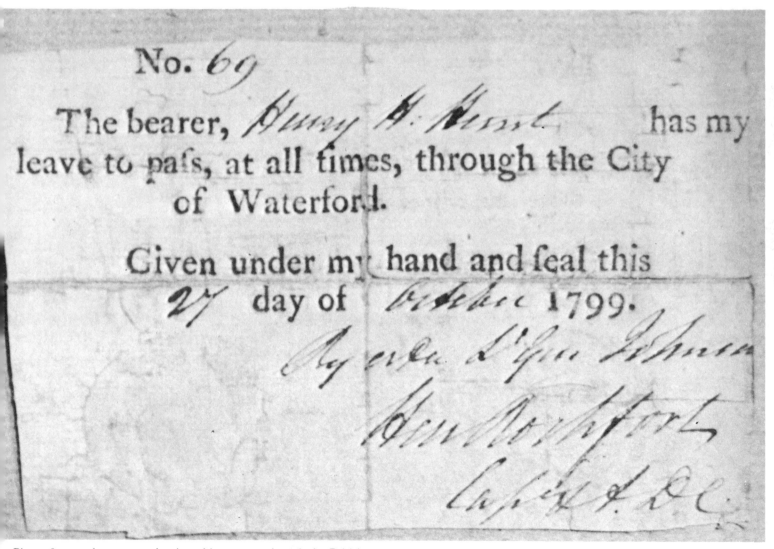

Piece of war ephemera: at the time this pass was issued, the British were still dealing with the aftermath of the Wolfe Tone rebellion and the attempted French invasion in Ireland.
90 × 131 mm

From the collector's point of view this is a particularly attractive
billhead, including as it does a finely engraved heading and a
completed, stamped and dated invoice.
126 × 204 mm

A car rear-window sticker protesting at the revived Channel road-tunnel project, which—if
ever completed—would link Kent, England with northern France.
63 × 230 mm

More war ephemera: a Road Traffic notice from the German
Occupying Force in Guernsey, Channel Islands.
328 × 200 mm

CHAPTER 1

The Great Days of the Horse

The horse has dominated the story of land travel and the movement of goods for centuries longer than any other mode of transport, but from the point of view of the ephemera collector, the golden age of the horse in Britain and Europe really begins after the mid-seventeenth century.

There are still very interesting printed or—more likely—handwritten papers to be found from the Tudor and early Stuart periods, and, of course, an exceptional stroke of luck might still turn up an even rarer document. A page of Anglo-Saxon farm accounts from Ely Abbey, including details of transportation of farm produce, which had survived in three pieces for nearly a thousand years until they were found and joined together again, sold at Sotheby's in London for £52,000 in 1979.

But it was not until people seriously began to rebuild a road system which, in Britain, had fallen very much into decay after Henry VIII's dissolution of the monasteries, that traffic could get moving in any quantity or speed. And once there were roads and traffic to move on them, pieces of paper were needed to keep the whole thing operating.

From the reign of Mary Tudor, when 'statute labour' was introduced, road repair was the responsibility of the local parish, and all parishioners, unless they could buy themselves out of the duty, had to give several days a year to working on the roads. However, the introduction of the turnpike system in the seventeenth century, brought a great change as far as main roads were concerned.

Under the turnpike system, stretches of road were enclosed and administered by trustees, who charged a fee to everyone using the road. Tollgates, 'bars' and turnstiles were set up at strategic points, forcing the traveller to stop and pay for a ticket which allowed passage to the next barrier, and sometimes on through a succession of such 'checkpoints'. The revenue so earned was intended to provide for the upkeep of the road, and for the payment of tollgate keepers and clerks, as well as leaving the board of trustees a profit. Each Turnpike Trust was set up by Act of Parliament, the first such act being passed in 1663. Under this act, the first tollgates to be erected outside London were put up on the Great North Road. A varying scale of charges was established, covering horses, coaches, waggons and animals—a halfpenny for twenty sheep, for instance, and five pence for twenty head of cattle.

In time, the country was covered with a network of thousands of miles of turnpike road, controlled by hundreds of boards of trustees. Many of the boards let out or auctioned their rights to sub-contractors, who did the actual work of gate-keeping. At the same time, minor roads remained the responsibility of the parish. The system lasted until the 1888 Local Government Act placed responsibility for roads on the new county councils and district councils.

Thus, for two centuries, during which Britain grew into a powerful industrial, manufacturing and exporting nation, the country's roads were built and repaired by a miscellaneous collection of committees, boards and councils. Some were efficient, some less so; some charged extortionate rates and a few were downright dishonest. But whatever its shortcomings, the turnpike system worked, and it is the great variety of paperwork created by its workings that provides the ephemera collector with a treasure-trove of social, historical and geographical commentary on life in Georgian and Victorian Britain.

Among paper throwaways directly related to the turnpike roads (rather than to the traffic that used them), are items covering the operation of the turnpike trustee: printed copies of the Act of Parliament which established them, notices of meetings (3), notices warning of the penalties for vandalism, or announcing lettings and auctions (4). Tables of charges displayed at the tollgate—and

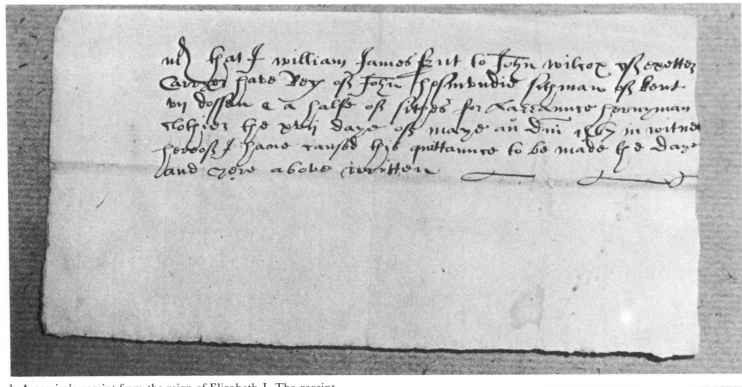

1. A carrier's receipt from the reign of Elizabeth I. The receipt reads: 'Witnessed that I, William James, servant to John Wilcox of Exetter, Carrier, have received of John Horsmondin Sithman of Kent, six dozen and a halfe of sithnes [scythes] for Lassanid Hornyman, Clothier, the seventeenth day of May anno domini 1567, in witness whereof I have caused this quittamur to be made the day and year above written'.
105 × 204 mm

2. A receipt for highway tax paid in 1747.

The 22 Day of *December* 1747

Received of *Mr Howard*
the Sum of *8 Shillings 4 pence* }
in full for 4 Quarter's Tax for the Highways of } *0 8 4*
the Parish of *St Annes*
due at *Christmas* last past. *next* }

By us *Wᵐ Howet* Surveyors.

TODMORDEN
Turnpike-Roads.

THE next Meeting of the Trustees for putting in Execution the Act of Parliament for Repairing the said Roads, will be on *Thursday* the *Twenty third* Day of *August* at Eleven o'Clock in the Forenoon, at the House of *Mr Wᵐ Murgatroyd, the Friendly Inn, in Warley.*

Hebden-Bridge,

Augᵗ 6 1827

By Order of the Trustees.

J. SUTCLIFFE, Clerk.

Printed at Chambers' Office, Todmorden.

3. Notice of a turnpike trustees' meeting, 1828.
205 × 165 mm

which were often the cause of angry altercation between the gatekeeper and those who wanted to pass through— and the tollgate tickets themselves (6) are mines of information. Such a collection may reveal the kind of traffic using the roads in various parts of the country, how charges differed from one area to another—even how the nature of the traffic changed, grew in volume or dwindled away over a period of years.

Of all the traffic on the turnpike roads, none plays a more romantic part in our folklore than the stage or post coach and its leaner, swifter cousin, the mail coach. But the coaching era did more than just supply us with a pretty subject for Christmas cards. In Georgian and early Victorian Britain, the stage and mail were the centre of an 'infrastructure' as complicated as any transport system today. The coaching business was subject to a large and ever-growing body of legislation and local government regulations.

For the coaches to operate efficiently there had to be a nationwide network of stables, inns, offices, repair yards; coachmakers, saddlers, harness-makers, blacksmiths and teams of postboys; suppliers of hay for horses, and food and drink for travellers; ostlers to look after the horses and waiters and maids to look after travellers. On the fringe of the business were hordes of tradesmen making—and more often than not advertising in picturesque style— everything from riding boots and spurs to conditioning powders and cures for rot in horses' feet.

The first stagecoaches—so-called because a 'stage' (about ten miles) was the distance a team of horses could travel before they had to be changed and rested—came into use in England around 1640. A quarter of a century later, though advertisements for stagecoaches had been appearing in English newspapers for some time, there were still only a handful of them in the whole country. By 1740, things had changed; roads were slowly getting better, though many public coaches still stopped running in the worst winter months, and the design and springing of coaches was much improved.

For the great majority of people who did not own their own carriages, there were livery and post stables where chaises could be hired, though this was relatively expensive. Several kinds of public coach were available: the post coach, which did not usually carry outside passengers; the stage, which could carry up to ten or eleven outside; and the mail coach.

The mail coach began operating in 1784, when the Government gave a contract to John Palmer, a Bath theatre manager, to carry mail on the Bristol Road. Be-

cause of their valuable loads, mail coaches carried armed guards and ran to regular, fast time-tables. Although more expensive than the stage, they very quickly became the more popular. The mail coaches reached their greatest glory in the reigns of George IV and William IV, but a few years into the reign of their niece, Victoria, the mail was virtually finished, killed off by the railway.

They left behind a vast amount of printed ephemera, much of it of great interest to the social historian as well as being among the most attractive of all transport ephemera.

Coach tickets are an obvious example. Stagecoach tickets were issued in triplicate, one section each for the passenger, the coach guard and the operator. They usually recorded the passenger's name, his destination, the name of the coach on which he wanted to travel, and whether he was booking an inside (more expensive) or outside seat. The passenger paid his fare to the guard at journey's end, usually adding a sizeable tip. Only the most exceptional luck will bring all three parts of a used stage coach ticket into a collector's hands, but individual sections may still be found.

The coach operators, most of whom had their booking offices at good quality inns, printed a wide selection of waybills, invoices and tickets for their own use. In addition they produced a great quantity of promotional material detailing all aspects of the business for the benefit of passengers: where and when coaches ran, journey times, towns served, distances between towns, fares, the amount of luggage a passenger might carry (usually between 14 and 20 pounds, at a cost of two or three pence per pound) and sometimes even notes in guidebook style concerning interesting items to look out for on the journey.

Much of this material was decorated with woodcut illustrations of coaches and horses, and the same stock illustrations often appeared on trade cards and notices of different coach or waggon operators, the jobbing printer using just one or two basic blocks, round which he would drop the names of individual coaches and operators.

The interested collector, bemused by this wealth of material, might well decide to limit his collecting to such specifics as ephemera carrying the names of coaching inns, or of the coaches themselves. This would still give him scope for collecting some lively material. Imagine a collection of posters, handbills, menu cards, bills and trade cards bearing such romantic inn names as the *Swan with Two Necks*, the *Belle Sauvage*, the *Bull and Mouth*, the *George*, the *White Bear* and the *Golden Cross*, or such splendid coach names as the *Stag*, the *Greyhound, Nimrod, Safety,*

Independence, *Telegraph*, and *Eclipse*.

Many coach operators also ran a fleet of waggons and flys for transporting goods, and some of the biggest waggon operators specialised wholly in the freight business and did not bother with passenger transport at all. Best-known among these, perhaps, is the international transport and removal company, Pickford, who began operating as carriers between London and Midland towns in the first half of the eighteenth century. Occasional early Pickford ephemera—an invoice or a waybill—may still be found on a fleamarket stall or in a forgotten trunk or attic box.

Although the coming of the railway spelt the end of the stage and mail coach, it could not so quickly oust the carrier's waggon. A well-established sight on England's roads from the early seventeenth century, the carrier's horse was still in use for this work in towns well into the twentieth century.

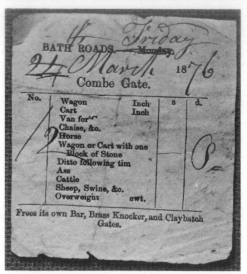

6. A group of tollgate tickets. The Wenlock and Westwood Gate ticket is unused, so still has both parts intact—one for the rider or driver, and one for the gatekeeper.
77 × 71 mm, 48 × 163 mm, 130 × 78 mm

Wenlock and Westwood Gate.			Wenlock and Westwood Gate.		
day of	184		day of	184	
	s.	d.		s.	d.
Horse			Horse		
Carriage and Horses			Carriage and Horses		
Frees Hill Top and Hazlar Gates.			Frees Hill Top and Hazlar Gates.		

ROUP OF TOLLS,
AND MEETING OF
ROAD TRUSTEES.

On Friday the 29th day of March, 1844, there will be Let, by Public Roup, within the Town-Hall of Kelso, at 12 o'Clock Noon, for One Year, from the 26th day of May, 1844, to the 26th day of May, 1845,

THE PONTAGES and TOLL-DUTIES payable at the following BARS, with the exception of the Toll or Pontage Duties exigible for Stage Coaches, which the Trustees reserve to be collected as they may direct, viz.:—

KELSO BRIDGE,	**SPROUSTON,**
TEVIOT BRIDGE,	**OLD VENCHEN,**
MAXTON,	**SHOTTON BURN,**
EDNAM,	AND
ROSEBANK,	**COWBOG.**
CARHAM BURN,	

Persons intending taking any of the Bars must bring their Securities to the Roup, otherwise their offers will not be received.

A Meeting of the Trustees, on the above Trust, will be held within the Clerk's Office, at Eleven o'Clock, for the purpose of adjusting the Articles of Roup, and for other business of the Trust.

KELSO, FEB. 29, 1844.

_____

KELSO: PRINTED BY ALEX. ELLIOT.

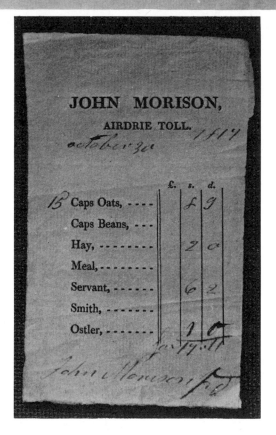

4. Notice of a letting by public roup (auction) of a list of toll bars around Kelso, Scotland. Many turnpike trusts, having won from Parliament the right to set up a turnpike, let them to others to save themselves the work and aggravations attendant on running the tolls. They still wanted to see a profit, however, as did the lessees—hence the high rates of toll in many parts of the country.
280 × 223 mm

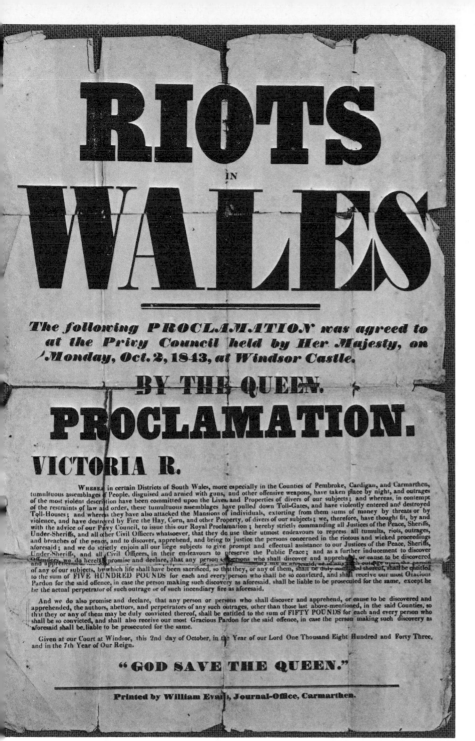

RIOTS
IN
WALES

The following PROCLAMATION was agreed to at the Privy Council held by Her Majesty, on Monday, Oct. 2, 1843, at Windsor Castle.

BY THE QUEEN.

PROCLAMATION.

VICTORIA R.

Whereas in certain Districts of South Wales, more especially in the Counties of Pembroke, Cardigan, and Carmarthen, tumultuous assemblages of People, disguised and armed with guns, and other offensive weapons, have taken place by night, and outrages of the most violent description have been committed upon the Lives and Properties of divers of our subjects; and whereas, in contempt of the restraints of law and order, these tumultuous assemblages have pulled down Toll-Gates, and have violently entered and destroyed Toll-Houses; and whereas they have also attacked the Mansions of individuals, extorting from them sums of money by threats or by violence, and have destroyed by Fire the Hay, Corn, and other Property, of divers of our subjects; we, therefore, have thought fit, by and with the advice of our Privy Council, to issue this our Royal Proclamation; hereby strictly commanding all Justices of the Peace, Sheriffs, Under-Sheriffs, and all other Civil Officers whatsoever, that they do use their utmost endeavours to repress all tumults, riots, outrages, and breaches of the peace, and to discover, apprehend, and bring to justice the persons concerned in the riotous and wicked proceedings aforesaid; and we do strictly enjoin all our liege subjects to give prompt and effectual assistance to our Justices of the Peace, Sheriffs, Under-Sheriffs, and all Civil Officers, in their endeavours to preserve the Public Peace; and as a further inducement to discover and apprehend the persons concerned therein, we do hereby promise and declare, that any person or persons who shall discover and apprehend, or cause to be discovered and apprehended, any person or persons, for any of the outrages aforesaid, or any such outrage, upon the perpetration of any of our subjects, by which life shall have been sacrificed, so that they, or any of them, shall be duly convicted thereof, shall be entitled to the sum of FIVE HUNDRED POUNDS for each and every person who shall be so convicted, and shall receive our most Gracious Pardon for the said offence, in case the person making such discovery as aforesaid, shall be liable to be prosecuted for the same, except he be the actual perpetrator of such outrage or of such incendiary fire as aforesaid.

And we do also promise and declare, that any person or persons who shall discover and apprehend, or cause to be discovered and apprehended, the authors, abettors, and perpetrators of any such outrage, other than those last above-mentioned, in the said Counties, so that they or any of them may be duly convicted thereof, shall be entitled to the sum of FIFTY POUNDS for each and every person who shall be so convicted, and shall also receive our most Gracious Pardon for the said offence, in case the person making such discovery as aforesaid shall be liable to be prosecuted for the same.

Given at our Court at Windsor, this 2nd day of October, in the Year of our Lord One Thousand Eight Hundred and Forty Three, and in the 7th Year of Our Reign.

"GOD SAVE THE QUEEN."

Printed by William Evans, Journal-Office, Carmarthen.

5. The men who ran the tollgates and turnpikes were often accused of dishonesty and extortion, accusations which erupted into violence in South Wales in 1842–3 in the 'Rebecca Riots', so-called in reference to Rebecca's descendants who would 'possess the gate of those which hate them' (Genesis 24.60). This notice proclaims the punishment to be meted out to the wreckers.
441 × 283 mm

9. This printed notice of the routes served by the coaches from the Royal Hotel, Cheltenham, emphasises the safety and elegance of the proprietor's post coaches.
165 × 144 mm

8. Trade card of an Ipswich coach operator.
75 × 111 mm

7. Trade card for coaches operating between London and Norwich, 1780s.
80 × 117 mm

10. The railway had not reached Blackpool in 1845 when the 'omnibus called *The Safety*', a forerunner of today's coach parties, ran there. The use of the word 'omnibus'—a horse-drawn vehicle for up to 20 people inside—is interesting here as the illustration shows an ordinary stage coach.
520 × 190mm

11. This trade card of a Kentish hotel emphasises the quality of its wines but does not forget to mention the coach horses.
90 × 136mm

13. Billhead of John Oak, the Castle Inn, Devizes, who hired out 'neat chaises'.
171 × 115mm

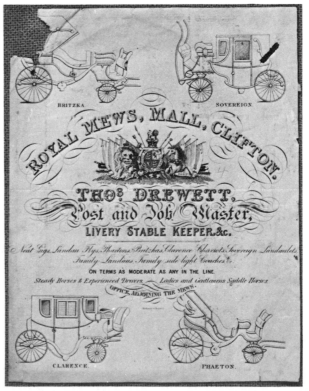

12. An ornate trade leaflet of a Bristol livery stable owner and coach proprietor—emphasises the quality of his product: 'moderate terms, steady horses and experienced drivers'—with a subtle hint at aristocratic patronage contained in the coat of arms.
220 × 172mm

14. According to this trade card, it took five days for a carrier to deliver goods from Glasgow to Carlisle in the 1780s. It is possible that the carrier did not travel on Sundays, however, as this was still an offence in some parts of the country.
92 × 165 mm

Twice a-week to CARLISLE.

BROUNS and HARKNESS, the CARLISLE-CARRIERS, depart from this City every Wednefday and Saturday, at four o'clock in the evening, and arrive at Carlifle on Monday and Thurfday the week following. The Moffat-Road, being nearly compleated, enables them to forward goods to London with more certainty, and is well known to be the fhorteft and cheapeft conveyance. It has been the cuftom to fend goods directed to Briftol, Exeter, Salifbury, and places adjacent, by way of London.

All goods for the above places, and places adjacent, directed to the care of JOHN HARGREAVES in Kendal, will be forwarded by him in fhorter time, and at much lefs expence than going by London, which muft be a confiderable faving upon goods to and from that quarter.

GLASGOW, Auguft 30th, 1781.

JAMES and THOMAS BROUN.
WILLIAM HARKNESS.
JOHN HARGREAVES.

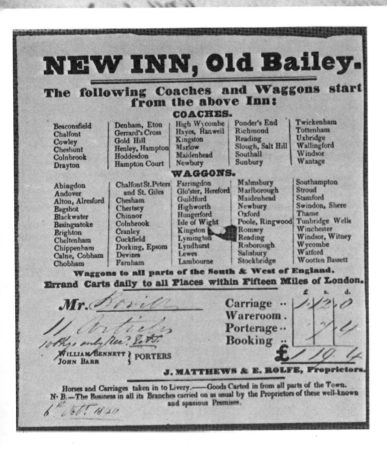

17. Saddle and harness maker's trade card.
90 × 61 mm

15. An invoice from a London coaching and waggon inn, the New Inn, Old Bailey, dated 1840.
150 × 133 mm

25

16. This delightful Victorian scrap takes coaching as its theme: the fashionable throng on the way to the Derby at Epsom.
90 × 315mm

THE ROAD TO THE DERBY: THE START.

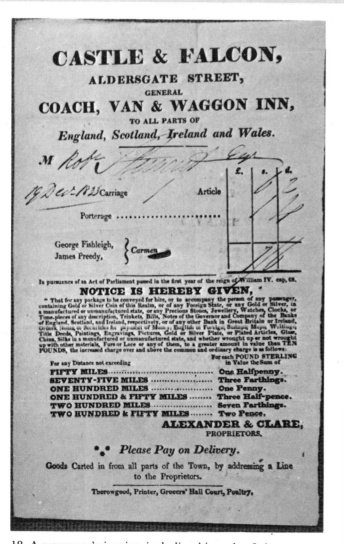

CASTLE & FALCON,
ALDERSGATE STREET,
GENERAL
COACH, VAN & WAGGON INN,
TO ALL PARTS OF
England, Scotland, Ireland and Wales.

M ....

.... Carriage .... Article

Porterage ....

George Fishleigh,   } Carmen
James Preedy,   }

In pursuance of an Act of Parliament passed in the first year of the reign of William IV. cap. 68.

NOTICE IS HEREBY GIVEN,

" That for any package to be conveyed for hire, or to accompany the person of any passenger, containing Gold or Silver Coin of this Realm, or of any Foreign State, or any Gold or Silver, in a manufactured or unmanufactured state, or any Precious Stones, Jewellery, Watches, Clocks, or Time-pieces of any description, Trinkets, Bills, Notes of the Governor and Company of the Banks of England, Scotland, and Ireland, respectively, or of any other Bank in Great Britain or Ireland, Orders, Notes, or Securities for payment of Money, English or Foreign, Stamps, Maps, Writings, Title Deeds, Paintings, Engravings, Pictures, Gold or Silver Plate, or Plated Articles, Glass, China, Silk is a manufactured or unmanufactured state, and whether wrought up or not wrought up with other materials, Furs or Lace or any of them, to a greater amount in value than TEN POUNDS, the increased charge over and above the common and ordinary charge is as follows:

For any Distance not exceeding	For each POUND STERLING in Value the Sum of
FIFTY MILES	**One Halfpenny.**
SEVENTY-FIVE MILES	**Three Farthings.**
ONE HUNDRED MILES	**One Penny.**
ONE HUNDRED & FIFTY MILES	**Three Half-pence.**
TWO HUNDRED MILES	**Seven Farthings.**
TWO HUNDRED & FIFTY MILES	**Two Pence.**

ALEXANDER & CLARE,
PROPRIETORS.

• *Please Pay on Delivery.*

Goods Carted in from all parts of the Town, by addressing a Line to the Proprietors.

Thorowgood, Printer, Grocers' Hall Court, Poultry.

18. A waggoner's invoice, including his scale of charges.
186 × 115mm

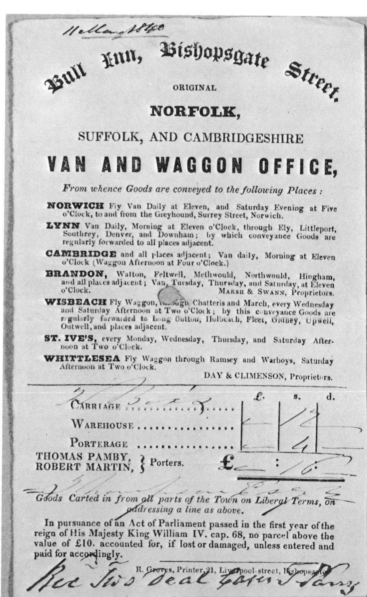

Bull Inn, Bishopsgate Street,
ORIGINAL
NORFOLK,
SUFFOLK, AND CAMBRIDGESHIRE
VAN AND WAGGON OFFICE,
From whence Goods are conveyed to the following Places :

NORWICH Fly Van Daily at Eleven, and Saturday Evening at Five o'Clock, to and from the Greyhound, Surrey Street, Norwich.

LYNN Van Daily, Morning at Eleven o'Clock, through Ely, Littleport, Southrey, Denver, and Downham; by which conveyance Goods are regularly forwarded to all places adjacent.

CAMBRIDGE and all places adjacent; Van daily, Morning at Eleven o'Clock (Waggon Afternoon at Four o'Clock).

BRANDON, Watton, Feltwell, Methwould, Northwould, Hingham, and all places adjacent; Van, Tuesday, Thursday, and Saturday, at Eleven o'Clock.   MARSH & SWANS, Proprietors.

WISBEACH Fly Waggon, through Chatteris and March, every Wednesday and Saturday Afternoon at Two o'Clock; by this conveyance Goods are regularly forwarded to Long Sutton, Holbeach, Fleet, Gidney, Upwell, Outwell, and places adjacent.

ST. IVE'S, every Monday, Wednesday, Thursday, and Saturday Afternoon at Two o'Clock.

WHITTLESEA Fly Waggon through Ramsey and Warboys, Saturday Afternoon at Two o'Clock.

DAY & CLIMENSON, Proprietors.

CARRIAGE ....   £. s. d.

WAREHOUSE ....

PORTERAGE ....

THOMAS PAMBY,   } Porters.   £ :
ROBERT MARTIN, }

Goods Carted in from all parts of the Town on Liberal Terms, on addressing a line as above.

In pursuance of an Act of Parliament passed in the first year of the reign of His Majesty King William IV. cap. 68, no parcel above the value of £10. accounted for, if lost or damaged, unless entered and paid for accordingly.

R. Groves, Printer, 21, Liverpool-street, Bishopsgate.

19. Van and Waggon office invoice, 1840.   192 × 120mm

21. Into the twentieth century, and this delivery service letterhead still emphasises the horse.
278 × 220 mm

22. Hired transport did not always require a horse: sedan chairs were still in use well into the nineteenth century. This is a printer's proof of an eighteenth-century sedan chair maker's trade card.
120 × 75 mm

20. An American Express money package.
100 × 240 mm

CHAPTER 2

TRANSPORT ON INLAND & COASTAL WATERS

Local water transport provides many interesting and attractive items for the ephemera collector, who may choose to range widely over the whole subject or confine himself (or herself) to one particular aspect. Canals alone could take him from the Manchester Ship Canal and the Regent's Park Canal in London to the Middle East and Suez, Panama or the achievements of the Dutch. If he stayed with rivers, he could become engrossed in the centuries-long story of the Thames as a commercial and holiday waterway, or in the shorter, but wonderfully vivid, history of the Show Boats of the Mississippi and Ohio Rivers. If he moved out to sea, but not too far from land, he might choose to concentrate on the great days of the pleasure steamer, on the work of collier brigs round Britain's coast, or even on the work of the men who guard shipping's interests on land—the coastguards, pilots and watermen.

Until comparatively recent times, water provided the medium for the quickest, cheapest and, sometimes, the only form of regular transport in many parts of the world. This was particularly true of Great Britain, whose 4,500-mile-long coast is enormous in relation to her relatively small land area, ensuring that Britain's coastal shipping would be an early feature of her transport history. Until the coming of the railways it was not the roads but the coastal seas, canals and navigable rivers of Great Britain that carried the bulk of the raw materials and finished products of her industrial revolution. Water transport had one outstanding advantage: economy. Half a dozen men in one boat could move a load on water which would need fifty waggons, each pulled by four horses and driven by two men, to shift on land. And in the period before the roads improved, the boat could almost always do it faster.

The canals of the eighteenth and nineteenth centuries play a particularly interesting part in the story of trans-port in Britain. The Romans had built several canals in Britain, and the Exeter Ship Canal was constructed in Elizabeth I's reign. But it remained for the Duke of Bridgewater, seeking a quick and cheap way to move coal from his mines at Worsley to nearby Manchester, to decide that canals like those he had seen in Holland and Belgium were the answer. It was in the middle of the eighteenth century that canal building began to catch the English imagination.

As with the turnpike roads, construction of canals in Britain required the sanction of an Act of Parliament. This gave canal promoters the right to buy land, construct the canal, collect tolls and keep it in good working order, at the same time imposing on them the obligation to allow suitable-sized craft to pass through the canal.

The 1759 Act, which allowed the Duke of Bridgewater and James Brindley, his brilliant engineer, to build their first canal, marked the beginning of a great increase in Britain's navigable inland waterways system that spanned the next seventy years or so.

Apart from the Bridgewater Navigations, which were to make their owner a very wealthy man indeed, canals were also built by joint-stock companies. So attractive was the prospect of the revenue to be gained from them that people with money to invest fell over each other in their eagerness to get in on a scheme. Shares were usually fully subscribed before a company's scheme received the sanction of Parliament. During the 'Canal Mania' of 1792–3, it was not unusual to hear tales of pandemonium at public meetings as people fought to get their names into the subscription books of the canal being proposed.

From the point of view of the ephemera collector, a drawback to all this exciting activity lies in the fact that very often the subscription book and the company's share register are the only records of proprietors' share

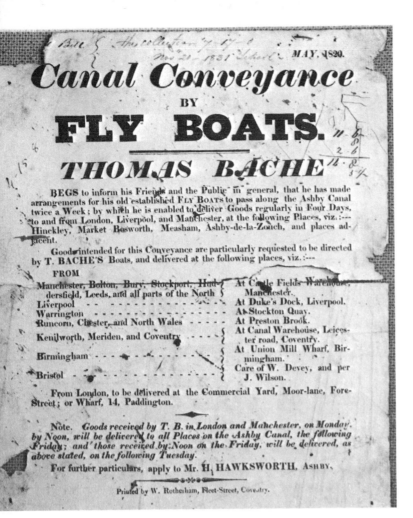

Canal Conveyance
BY
FLY BOATS.
THOMAS BACHE

BEGS to inform his Friends and the Public in general, that he has made arrangements for his old established FLY BOATS to pass along the Ashby Canal twice a Week; by which he is enabled to deliver Goods regularly in Four Days, to and from London, Liverpool, and Manchester, at the following Places, viz.:— Hinckley, Market Bosworth, Measham, Ashby-de-la-Zouch, and places adjacent.

Goods intended for this Conveyance are particularly requested to be directed by T. BACHE'S Boats, and delivered at the following places, viz.:—

FROM	
Manchester, Bolton, Bury, Stockport, Huddersfield, Leeds, and all parts of the North	At Castle Fields Warehouse, Manchester.
Liverpool	At Duke's Dock, Liverpool.
Warrington	At Stockton Quay.
Runcorn, Chester, and North Wales	At Preston Brook.
Kenilworth, Meriden, and Coventry	At Canal Warehouse, Leicester road, Coventry.
Birmingham	At Union Mill Wharf, Birmingham.
Bristol	Care of W. Devey, and per J. Wilson.

From London, to be delivered at the Commercial Yard, Moor-lane, Fore-Street; or Wharf, 14, Paddington.

Note. Goods received by T. B. in London and Manchester, on Monday by Noon, will be delivered to all Places on the Ashby Canal, the following Friday; and those received by Noon on the Friday, will be delivered, as above stated, on the following Tuesday.

For further particulars, apply to Mr. H. HAWKSWORTH, ASHBY.

Printed by W. Rotherham, Fleet-Street, Coventry.

2. Using canals for delivering freight: the notice of a carrier operating on the Ashby Canal, Leicestershire.
239 × 201 mm

1. Notice of proposed rates for the Rochdale canal, June 1846.
250 × 200 mm

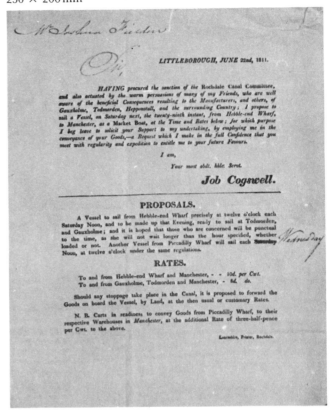

LITTLEBOROUGH, JUNE 22nd, 1811.

HAVING procured the sanction of the Rochdale Canal Committee, and also actuated by the warm persuasions of many of my Friends, who are well aware of the beneficial Consequences resulting to the Manufacturers, and others, of Gauxholme, Todmorden, Heppenstall, and the surrounding Country, I propose to sail a Vessel, on Saturday next, the twenty-ninth instant, from Hebble-end Wharf, to Manchester, as a Market Boat, at the Time and Rates below; for which purpose I beg leave to solicit your Support to my undertaking, by employing me in the conveyance of your Goods,—a Request which I make in the full Confidence that you meet with regularity and expedition to entitle me to your future Favours.

I am,

Your most obdt. hble. Servt.

Job Cogswell.

PROPOSALS.

A Vessel to sail from Hebble-end Wharf precisely at twelve o'clock each Saturday Noon, and to be made up that Evening, ready to sail at Todmorden, and Gauxholme; and it is hoped that those who are concerned will be punctual to the time, as she will not wait longer than the hour specified, whether loaded or not. Another Vessel from Piccadilly Wharf will sail each Saturday Noon, at twelve o'clock under the same regulations.

RATES.

To and from Hebble-end Wharf and Manchester, - - 10d. per Cwt.
To and from Gauxholme, Todmorden and Manchester, - 8d. do.

Should any stoppage take place in the Canal, it is proposed to forward the Goods on board the Vessel, by Land, at the then usual or customary Rates.

N. B. Carts in readiness to convey Goods from Piccadilly Wharf, to their respective Warehouses in Manchester, at the additional Rate of three-half-pence per Cwt. to the above.

Leicester, Printer, Rochdale.

THE SEVERN COMMISSION.

REGULATIONS as to vessels navigating on the River Severn during the period of War.

1. Port and starboard navigation lights, stern lights and headlamps to be dimmed and screened in the manner approved by the Chief Constables of Gloucestershire, Worcestershire and the City of Worcester.
2. All lights in cabins must be screened so as not to show any light outside.
3. On receiving an air raid warning, all lights must be extinguished.
4. Sirens are to be used only when essential for navigation purposes, and signals must be as short as possible.
5. In the event of an air raid warning, all vessels in locks or lock cuttings must proceed out of such locks or lock cuttings, and no vessel will be allowed to moor in the vicinity of a lock.
6. Vessels, during the period of an air raid warning, may be halted in the open country, and, unless the crew remain on board, must be properly and securely moored to the bank in positions not likely to cause danger to other vessels or property.
7. In the event of an air raid warning any vessels passing through towns or built-up areas, or passing any warehouses, buildings, petroleum or other depots, must proceed with all speed.
8. Vessels tied up at quays and wharves when an air raid warning is sounded should generally remain in such positions until the all clear signal is given.
9. In case a vessel passes through a gas attack and is in danger of contamination, it must be stopped at the first lock and a report made to the Lock-keeper, who will at once communicate with the local A.R.P. Official.
10. To facilitate detection of blister gases, it is suggested that all traders using the Navigation should be prepared to provide their vessels with small boards, say 18 inches square, treated with either detector paint or detector painted paper, the boards being fixed, e.g. as under:—
    One near the fore-end.
    One near the middle beam.
    One near the aft-end.

By order of the Severn Commissioners,

Bank Buildings, Cross, Worcester. 2nd October, 1939.

J. LIONEL WOOD, Clerk.

SPECIFICATION OF APPROVED LIGHTS.

THE GREAT YARMOUTH PORT & HAVEN ACTS
1866 TO 1911.

Tolls Payable on the River Bure.

JAMES PUMFREY,
Collector,
North Quay,
Great Yarmouth.

Mr Harold Percival

DATE.	NAME OF WHERRY.	OR YACHT.	AMOUNT DUE.		
			£	s.	d.
1914	To Register Toll				
Reg No 2224 Unknown				10	0

RECEIVED
8 JAN 1915

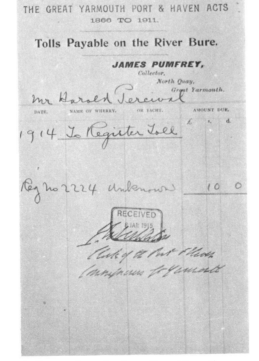

SUMMER TRIPS
THROUGH 90 MILES OF THAMES SCENERY
OXFORD TO KINGSTON

SEASON 1928.
Saloon Steamers run daily
(SUNDAYS EXCEPTED) Between
Oxford, Wallingford, Henley, Windsor, Kingston.
MAY 17th to SEPTEMBER 29th, 1928.

For further particulars see Steamer Guide and Time Table—Post free Threepence.

SALTER BROS., Limited,
FOLLY BRIDGE, OXFORD.

Please keep for reference.

4. Stamped receipt for tolls paid on the River Bure, which flows into the Yare at Great Yarmouth, in 1914.
210 × 130 mm

6. An elegant steamer on the Thames graces this 1928 trade card from Salter Brothers, who still run pleasure boats on the river.
138 × 68 mm

3. The effects of war on river traffic. This notice sets out the special regulations to be observed by shipping on the River Severn, during World War II.

holdings; share certificates were not generally issued by corporations until the canal-building age was well advanced.

But this still leaves many other papers of interest connected with the canal-building boom: notices and advertisements announcing public meetings for or against canal projects (1); official notices listing toll charges and freight rates; rules and regulations governing the use of the canals; toll tickets, bills and invoices; and the trade cards and bills of boatmen and carriers.

Much of the ephemera relating to canals is equally relevant to, or overlaps with, that generated by river users. Users of both required the services of boat builders, repairers and marine suppliers, were obliged to obey rules and regulations (3) and had to pay tolls and dues (4).

As the nineteenth century turned into the twentieth, the traffic became more and more devoted to pleasure, and commercial uses of canals and rivers gradually disappeared. By the 1960s, the great stream of craft—West Country barges, narrow boats, and Thames barges—which had used the Thames from Lechlade to the Pool of London, had virtually disappeared. Their cargoes—timber, chalk, bricks, farm produce, coal from Somerset via the Kennet and Avon Canal, Huntley and Palmer's biscuits and Simmonds' India Pale Ale from Reading, or brandy made from beetroot and bound for France from Buscot—had found new routes.

The new traffic using Britain's rivers and canals generated 'ephemera of pleasure': the business cards of boat hirers and proprietors of pleasure launches (6); tide tables and river maps, some of them very decorative; the brochures of waterside pubs and hotels and lists of goods supplied by marine service shops and boat basins.

Coastal shipping saw similar changes. First the railways, and in our own time the building of motorway systems used by giant transporter lorries, have changed the nature of transport the world over. But even before the railways, the steam engine had brought about a revolution in coast shipping.

As with the canals, this change was particularly marked in Great Britain. For centuries, coastal trade in British waters had been dominated by the shipping of coal and grain, carried in brigs like the *John and Thomas* (7). Scores of small ports owed their livelihoods, if not their very existence, to this trade. Early in the nineteenth century came the steam engine, first commercially successful

in boats—not at sea but on the Clyde in Scotland. By 1815, the year of Waterloo, there were about a dozen steamships in action on the Clyde, and down on the Thames the first steamship passenger services had been started between London and Gravesend. They grew rapidly, turning small places like Margate into holiday towns visited by hundreds of thousands of Londoners each year, and causing many a coastal hotel or inn to point out its proximity to a steamship landing stage rather than to a coaching office (8).

Steamships were popular because they were quicker than sailing ships and not having to depend on wind and tide, were distinctly more reliable. In their early days they were also cheaper than coaches. They transformed passenger travel between Glasgow and Northern Ireland and between northern England and Scotland. By the middle of the century, much coastal shipping had been converted to steam and most steamships, even if they were engaged primarily in cargo trade, carried a few passengers as well.

The volume of coastal trade in British waters was enormous throughout the nineteenth century. It was not until half way through Edward VII's reign that the volume of cargo reaching Britain's ports from her Empire and other foreign countries exceeded in tonnage the cargo coming in from her own coastal trade.

Clearly, the printed ephemera resulting from business on this scale is wide-ranging and varied in subject matter and style. It is only possible to hint at the wealth of material available.

Among the most attractive items are the posters, sailing notices, trade cards and timetable brochures of steamship companies, with their lively engravings of ships, usually depicted as flag-bedecked and at full steam ahead. Bill heads can also be very decorative. An example is the receipt from the Philadelphia Steam Propeller Company's Swiftsure Line (16) and even if these were simply printed and decorated, as with the receipt for the bundle carried on the steamboat *Bunker Hill* in 1838 (17), they may retain a certain elegance of style.

As well as the ephemera which might come the way of a passenger—tickets, dining saloon menus and baggage labels—there are the purely business items. The administration side of coastal and river shipping provides many interesting pieces, including pilot levies, apprentice indenture certificates, employer contracts and bills of lading.

8. The engraving on this trade card gives the impression that Back's London Hotel in Dover (spelt Dovor here) had the steam packets coming up to its front door. Dover was, of course, a cross-Channel port rather than a local coastal resort.

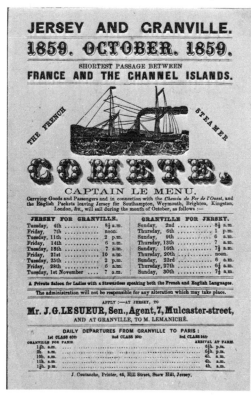

JERSEY AND GRANVILLE.
1859. OCTOBER. 1859.
SHORTEST PASSAGE BETWEEN
FRANCE AND THE CHANNEL ISLANDS.

THE FRENCH STEAMER

COMETE.
CAPTAIN LE MENU.

11. A French steamer, the *Comète*, features in this 1859 timetable for a steamer service between Jersey and Granville, Normandy.

9. Front cover of a Glasgow steamer operator's timetable for the Scottish islands in 1926.
180 × 121 mm

The Royal Route
TO THE
Western Highlands
AND
Islands of Scotland

TOURIST PROGRAMME
AND
TIME TABLE
(MAY TO SEPTEMBER)
Of the Royal Mail Steamers of
DAVID MACBRAYNE, LTD.
119 HOPE STREET, GLASGOW, C.2.
1926.

To be SOLD, by Public Auction,
On MONDAY the 30th of *June*, 1794,
At the House of Mrs. ANN BUCKHAM, in KING-STREET, WHITEHAVEN,
The good BRIGANTINE called the

JOHN and THOMAS,

THOMAS FANNING, Master, who is quitting the Sea;

Burthen One Hundred and Seventy Six Tons per Register; will take One Hundred and Fifteen Waggons of Coals, at about Twelve Feet Six Inches Water; sails and takes the Ground remarkably well; had a thorough Repair in August, 1792, in which there was upwards of Four Hundred Pounds expended. She is from Five Feet Six Inches to Six Feet throughout between Decks, and stands well on the Underwriters Books; can continue in the Coal Trade without a Shilling being laid out, and go on any Foreign Voyage at a small Expence.

The Purchaser to pay Twenty Guineas in Hand, and give approved Security when struck, for the Remainder at Three and Six Months, or the Deposit forfeited.

*** All Persons, having Claims against the said Vessel, are requested to send in their Accounts to Mr. WILLIAM STITT, in Roper-street.

STEAM BETWEEN LONDON AND NEWCASTLE
TWICE — A-WEEK.
THE SCREW STEAM SHIPS
SENTINEL AND BRIGADIER
WITH SPLENDID ACCOMMODATION FOR PASSENGERS
FROM IRONGATE STEAM WHARF, LONDON,
every Wednesday and Saturday evening at Six o'clock
and from LONDON WHARF, NEWCASTLE, every Wednesday and Saturday.
1863
William Davies Stephens

10. Trade card of a steamer company operating between London and Newcastle.
88 × 130 mm

7. This auction sale notice for the collier brig *John and Thomas* is of particular interest because it includes an inventory of everything to be sold with her, from anchor cables, sails, carpenter's tools and water casks to the ship's bell and a 'few pieces of beef'.
376 × 314 mm

13. Poster announcing the decision of the
Aberdeen and London Steam Navigation
Company to call at Sunderland, April 1835.
445 × 283 mm

12. Sea travel between the Channel Islands and
the French coast in 1978: the elegant steamer
has long since given way to the motor vessel and
the hydrofoil. Front cover of the timetable of
Condor, a Company based in St. Peter Port,
Guernsey.
209 × 102, unfolding to 209 × 505 mm

17. Receipt for freight carried on an American
steamboat, the *Bunker Hill*, in 1838.
78 × 184 mm

Steam Conveyance
BETWEEN
Sunderland & London.

THE
Aberdeen and London
Steam Navigation Company

Beg to intimate to the Public of Sunderland, Newcastle, North and
South Shields, Durham, and Neighbourhood, that they have made
arrangements for their powerful and splendid Steam Vessels, the

Duke of Wellington
AND
Queen of Scotland,

Of 200 Horse-power each,

to call in Sunderland Roads weekly, on their passages to and from
London ; to take on board and land Passengers and light Goods at
Sunderland.

The Duke of Wellington,
FOR LONDON,

will call in the Roads on Sunday the 12th inst. between 4 and 5
o'Clock, afternoon. Passengers intending to go by that Vessel will
have to go on board a clean comfortable Steam Boat, which will be in
attendance at Thornhill's Quay, Sunderland, at half-past 3 o'Clock,
to be conveyed to the Roads.

For particulars apply to
DAVID SHIRREFS,

Sunderland, April 8th, 1835.   *17, Nile Street, Sunderland.*

E. SMITH, PRINTER, SUNDERLAND.

16. To the twentieth-century eye, the ornate handwriting is probably as interesting an aspect of this receipt as its design and text.
312 × 252 mm

18. Some of America's fastest clippers were built in Baltimore, whose port figures in the illustration on the cover of the Atlantic Deeper Inland Waterways 1908 banquet menu.
311 × 253 mm

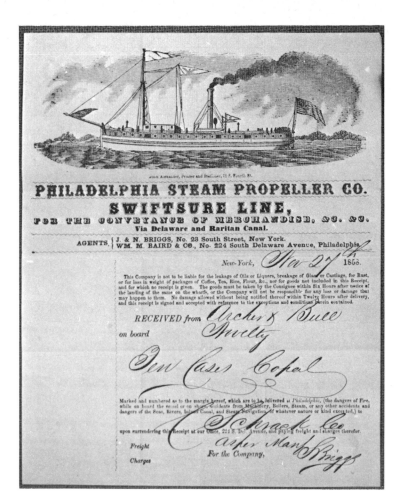

15. The sinking of the *Princess Alice* in the Thames in 1878 was a disaster whose horror caught the public imagination in the same way as the Tay Bridge collapse in Scotland, and was the subject of poems and popular prints, such as this. The *Princess Alice* was rammed by a collier, the *Bywell Castle*, and sank in five minutes. 650 bodies were recovered from the river.
230 × 171 mm

CHAPTER 3

THE RAILWAY AGE

There can be little doubt that the railway industry provides one of the richest hunting grounds for the collector of transport ephemera, for it engages millions of people world-wide and affects almost every facet of human endeavour. Inevitably this produces a vast quantity of printed paper.

In the early days of haphazard development, when a railway-mad public could be persuaded to support almost every railway line proposed, however short or unsuitable, railway company share certificates were as common as confetti at a wedding. Not all of them were as elaborate as the one for the Boston Elevated Railway, (1) but their holders believed in them as firmly as they believed in the ultimate virtues of material progress. Even the collapse of English 'Railway King' George Hudson, whose skill at buying up smaller railway lines and increasing their dividends finally came unstuck in 1849, did not deter them and the railway mania went on throughout the third quarter of the century in Britain and elsewhere beyond that time.

This optimism was a characteristic of the successful middle-class Victorian who, like Voltaire's Candide, thought that everything was for the best in the best of all possible worlds. The attitude was hardly shared by the workers who, managed in gangs by labour entrepreneurs, often found themselves obliged to spend their money at an appointed shop owned by the entrepreneur himself, and were therefore never out of debt to him. Attempts, by the railway companies, to prevent this practice (2) had little success. Intimidation by other railway company thugs, or by labour leaders who used bullying tactics to persuade workers to strike was another hazard for the individual worker, though this too aroused protest (3). The Hartlepool Dock and Railway Company offered ten guineas for information on anyone trying to intimidate the work force. Identification of the culprit would have meant no further work with the company. There is no means of telling whether the company was attempting to ensure a supply of cheap labour or whether the intimidators were representing the genuine interests of the workers.

Alongside the business of running the lines themselves, the locomotive and coach building industry was busily evolving new models for rival companies. Fierce competition in the latter part of the century obliged the railway companies to try to outdo each other in the comforts and elegance of their rolling stock. Thus were introduced the restaurant car, the sleeping car and the American Pullman car, whose main rival in Europe was the sleeping car introduced by Georges Nagelmackers, creator of the famous Wagons-Lits company. Not all railway car builders were successful, however, as was the case with the Jewett Car Company of Newark, Ohio, whose bid was turned down.

Investors in the railway business naturally expected to see profit from their support of the new means of transport and it was the duty of the company's managers to see that this was forthcoming. This was not easy. It was essential, therefore, that a line should get off to a good start and the opening of a new service was advertised widely. The Stockton and Darlington Railway, on which the first steam passenger engines operated, advertised the running of new railway coaches between St. Helen's Auckland and Darlington in 1836 (5) and the Great North of England Railway announced its birth in 1841 with services from Darlington to York (6).

The next decade saw the railway lines threading their way across all parts of the world and the companies that built them proliferated in bewildering confusion. The first German railways were established in 1835, the Austrian

1. The early days of railway mania led to the floating of innumerable companies to exploit the new form of transport. Not all of the railways remained solvent. This more recent certificate is for shares in the Boston Elevated Railway and the shares were worth $100 each. In America the Vanderbilts and Morgans were among the people who became successful railway barons.
195 × 289 mm

2. The system by which railworkers were obliged to spend their pay at the store by the employer was not approved of by all railway companies. In this notice the Stockton and Darlington Railway warn that they will not use contractors who do not give their workers the freedom to spend their wages as and where they like.
250 × 190 mm

3. Though there was some attempt to persuade workers to withhold their work in order to force the employer to pay higher wages the workforce, composed of tough, independent minded 'navvies' was difficult to organise. Nevertheless the railway felt it necessary to offer a reward for information about anyone trying to persuade the workers to strike.

in 1838, Italy followed in 1839 and Switzerland in 1844, with Spain introducing the broad-gauge track (still in operation today) in 1848.

In Britain, there were so many companies issuing their own tickets, that life for the passenger could be difficult indeed, though this very complexity is a source of continual interest to the ephemerist who specialises in tickets.

Initially the railway companies issued their tickets as paper coupons which were entered in a ledger by the booking clerk. This cumbersome system gave way to the counterfoil ticket, the stub of which remained in the possession of the issuer. All tickets carried the passenger's name and details of the train on which he was travelling. As rail traffic grew even this system proved to be impractical and too labour-intensive, though it continued to be used for long journeys involving several railway companies until late in the nineteenth century. In 1837 Thomas Edmondson, a clerk on the Newcastle and Carlisle Railway, had the happy notion of creating a small pasteboard ticket for simple journeys on a specific railway company. These were dated and numbered by a press and thus saved an enormous amount of booking-office time, as well as simplifying the accountancy process. This type of ticket (8) has survived until the present day and its number and variety has demanded a thorough knowledge of the railway systems by ticket clerks. More recently, experiments have been made in developing electronic ticket-issuing machines which automatically stamp all the details of the journey on a large and thinner type of card. This has produced a new type of ticket which is gradually taking over from the century-old pasteboard invention of Thomas Edmondson—at least at the larger terminals.

For the ephemera collector, railway tickets are one of the most fascinating items of railway documentation. Not only do the tickets represent the ideas and development of the diverse railway companies that existed throughout the length and breadth of Britain, but they reflect the intense rivalry that existed between them. This competitive spirit gave rise to innumerable variations on the basic ticket—the class structure that provided different fares for varying degrees of comfort and service; the 'special offer' tickets for holidays, day and week excursions, season tickets, party tickets, rover tickets and even tickets for dogs.

Another fascinating area of railway literature is the timetable. Like the ticket, it reached its threshold of development when railway traffic had increased to a level which made its publication not only desirable but economically viable. Before the 1830s, railway companies did not feel it necessary to do more than publish leaflets giving a broad description of their routes. This was often accompanied by a map, showing the stops en route (but not times of arrival), and claims that the route, for example, between Glasgow, Liverpool and London is 'the most picturesque'.

The beginning of the timetable as we know it today, dates back to a slim publication by George Bradshaw named the *Railway Time Table and Assistant to Railway Travel*. This appeared in 1839 and included fares and maps, as well as times of arrival and departure. As the railways developed, timetables became larger and more elaborate—so much so that their contents were almost beyond the comprehension of the ordinary layman, who would find it difficult to decipher the complications of routes, times, make-up of trains, change-over points and so on. The problem became acute where foreign railway travel was concerned and no doubt it was this that gave Thomas Cook the idea of publishing a simplified *Continental Timetable* in 1873.

Cook's Timetable gradually added to its contents other information of use to the traveller and in its present form it contains timetables of all the main railways throughout the world, as well as maps, temperature charts, currency guides, lists of consular offices and other useful information for travellers.

In their heyday the railways exerted themselves to provide ever more luxurious services to their passengers. Each company published its own literature, adding a rich vein to this field of railway ephemera. Restaurant cars were advertised by handbills and those who used them were given often elegant menus and tempting lists of wines (16a). The most splendid of these were provided on the great European services of the Wagons-Lits company, whose luxurious trains included the Orient Express, the Leningrad-Lisbon Express and the Blue Train.

Railway companies also extended their catering arrangements beyond the railway lines and built imposing hotels to house their travellers. The Wagons-Lits company owned a chain of splendid 'Palace' hotels among which were the Pera Palace at Istanbul and an hotel in Peking built for travellers on the Trans-Siberian Express. British Railway companies also built magnificent hotels at their major termini. Notable among these were the Euston Hotel (16) and the neo-gothic Midland masterpiece at St. Pancras.

STOCKTON & DARLINGTON RAILWAY

COACHES.

Increased Accommodation.

SUMMER OF 1836,

Commencing March 15th.

Separate Engines having been appointed for the Conveyance of Passengers and Merchandize, and a Coach attached to the latter Train, the Opportunities of Communication between the Towns of Darlington and Stockton are doubled, and between Darlington and Shildon they are now four times a-day.

DARLINGTON and St. HELEN'S AUCKLAND TRAIN.

Fares : Inside, 1s. 6d.—Outside, 1s. 3d., each way.

STATIONS.	TIMES OF STARTING.	STATIONS.	TIMES OF STARTING.
SHILDON, at	-	From DARLINGTON, at	half past 8 o'clock.
St. HELEN'S AUCKLAND	quarter bef. 7	Do.	half past 1
Do.	11	Do.	half past 5
Do.	quarter bef. 4	Do. to SHILDON	8

from the LANDS at a Quarter past 6 in the Morning, and from DARLINGTON to the LANDS at Half past 5 in the Evening.

N. B. The Train will leave Shildon half an hour after leaving St. Helen's Auckland. A CAR from Bishop Auckland to St. Helen's or New Shildon, meets each of these Trains in going and returning.

Fares to Shildon : Inside, 1s.—Outside, 9d.

DARLINGTON and STOCKTON TRAIN.

First-class Fares : Inside 2s.—Outside, 1s. 6d., each way.

Second-class, or Merchandize Fares : Inside, 1s. 6d.—Outside, 1s., each way.

From DARLINGTON,		TIMES OF STARTING	From STOCKTON, at		TIMES OF STARTING
	(Merchandize) at	half past 6 o'clock			quarter past 7 o'clock.
Do.		half past 8	Do.	(Merchandize)	9
Do.	(Merchandize)	11	Do.		quarter bef. 12
Do.		half past 1	Do.	(Merchandize)	1
Do.	(Merchandize)	3	Do.		quarter past 4
Do.		half past 5	Do.	(Merchandize)	half past 6

MONDAYS and WEDNESDAYS, a Second-class, or One Shilling Carriage, will accompany the First-class Coach Train.

STOCKTON and MIDDLESBRO' TRAIN.

Fares ; Inside, 6d.—Outside, 4d., each way.

MIDDLESBRO' at	TIMES	From STOCKTON, at	TIMES
	half past		half past 7 o'clock.
Do.	half past 8	Do.	half past 9
Do.	11	Do.	half past 11
Do.	half past 12	Do.	half past 1
Do.	2	Do.	half past 2
Do.	half past 3	Do.	half past 4
Do.	6	Do.	half past 6
Do.	7	Do.	half past 7

the Darlington and Middlesbro' Trains are in immediate connexion with each other, excepting those marked thus ✱

The MERCHANDIZE TRAIN will be allowed from One and a Half to Two Hours between Darlington and Stockton, whilst various applications having been made by Gentlemen in the Neighbourhood, to have the Coach Trains expedited and improved, Arrangements have been made to run the Darlington and Stockton Trip in FORTY-FIVE MINUTES, a New Engine and Outside Coach are provided, and the Fares now charged for this Class are consequently about on the par of other Railways.

All PARCELS (requiring haste and care), are to be left as under :—

THOMAS REYNOLDS, Angel Inn, Bishop Auckland   JAMES TURNER, Northgate Darlington
COXON, St. Helen's Auckland   GEORGE PEACOCK, Majestic Office, Stockton
THOMPSON, New Shildon   JOHN UNTHANK, Middlesbro'

GENERAL MERCHANDIZE for all Parts of the Kingdom, to R. ROBINSON, Merchandize Station, Darlington.

Railway Office, Darlington, March 4th, 1836.

COATES AND FARMER, PRINTERS, DARLINGTON.

5. The Stockton and Darlington Railway began to operate in 1825 and managed to maintain its independence until 1863 when it was absorbed by the North Eastern. Extension of services as advertised in this handbill was essential to survival.
225 × 190 mm

The passenger side was only one aspect of the railway business. Though more glamorous than freight, passenger traffic cannot equal the carriage of goods in the volume of documentation and collectible ephemera.

Documents needed for the despatch of goods, insurance, and receipts for collection, correspondence relating to the transport of goods and even special publications giving news about railway freight (20) are all part of the rich store of freight literature. Much of it in recent times has been thrown away in a countrywide spring clean that has destroyed many of the items that gave actuality and life to railway history. Some of it, happily, survives.

Much of the ephemera of the railways had a high artistic value. Typical are the posters, now treasured at museums, especially at the Railway Museum in York and at the Victoria and Albert Museum in London, and commemorative publications celebrating the opening of a new line or the anniversary of an old one.

On a minor scale, the ephemera collector may come across many other fragments of the history of the railways. Among these are give-aways such as calendars, broadsheets containing instructions to railway staff, printed public notices and even luggage labels such as the one specially printed for the Duke of Wellington's servant (17).

Despite their enormous influence and undoubted success, the railways have not found life easy during the one hundred and fifty years since passenger rail travel began on the Liverpool and Manchester Railway.

The early years of struggle to remain solvent in the face of escalating cost; labour difficulties; unforeseen problems arising from the nature of the land traversed, and objections from those who lived on it—all are recorded in strike notices, bankruptcy orders, protest handbills and other ephemeral documents.

In one handbill, signed 'Humanitas', the publisher is evidently on the side of the railway and against those who are opposing its intention to build a level crossing at Peterborough. 'Gentlemen, Spare you humanity,' it exclaims, 'since you will not extend it. The evil you sign against is most problematical; the good you would oppose most positive'. Such stirring documents, echoed in modern times by handbills designed to save lines from extinction (22), evoke the glories of the railway age with all its expansionist optimism and its determination to prevail. For the collector of ephemera the printed paper that remains as evidence of this golden age provides a thrill of actuality which no written account can equal.

6. The Great North of England Railway began its life as a service for carrying minerals and started passenger services from York to Darlington in March 1841. It was later incorporated in the North Eastern.
280 × 220 mm

OPENING

OF THE

Great North of England RAILWAY.

The Public are informed that the GREAT NORTH OF ENGLAND RAILWAY will be opened from York to Darlington, for Public Traffic, on *WEDNESDAY*, the 31st March, 1841.

The Trains will depart at the following Hours :—

FROM DARLINGTON TO YORK.

5·45 a.m.—taking Passengers for London, Derby, Birmingham, Sheffield, and Manchester.

8 a.m.—taking Passengers for London, Derby, Birmingham, Sheffield, Manchester, Leeds, Selby, and Hull.

12·30 p.m.—taking Passengers for Derby, Sheffield, Manchester, Leeds, Selby, and Hull.

3 p.m.—(MAIL,) taking Passengers for London, Derby, Leicester, Birmingham, Sheffield, Manchester, Leeds, Selby, and Hull.

6 p.m.—taking Passengers to York.

FROM YORK TO DARLINGTON.

6 a.m.—bringing passengers from York.

7·20 a.m.—(MAIL,) bringing Passengers from London, Leicester, Derby, and Sheffield.

9·35 a.m.—bringing Passengers from Manchester, Leeds, Selby, and Hull.

2·30 p.m.—bringing Passengers from Birmingham, Derby, Sheffield, Manchester, Leeds, Selby, and Hull.

6 p.m.—bringing Passengers from London, Birmingham, Derby, Sheffield, Manchester, Leeds, Selby, and Hull.

Until further notice, Passengers will only be booked as far as York, where the Carriages are changed.

Until the 6th of April, 1841, the London Mail Trains will leave York at 8·15 a.m., instead of the hours stated in the Time Table.

FARES BETWEEN YORK AND DARLINGTON :

PASSENGERS.		CARRIAGES.		HORSES.		
1st Class.	2nd Class.	On 2 Wheels.	On 4 Wheels.	One.	Two.	Three.
12s.	9s.	20s.	30s.	20s.	30s.	36s.

Parties riding in their own Carriages, and Children under 7 years of age, at lower rates.

Carriages and Horses must be at the Station a quarter of an hour before the departure of the Trains ; and, to prevent disappointment, previous notice should be given at the Station.

The Company will not be responsible for Luggage, unless it is booked and paid for according to its value ; and Passengers are particularly requested to have their name and address fully marked thereon, and to satisfy themselves that it is deposited on the Carriages.

(1)

J. & J. READMAN, PRINTERS, DARLINGTON.

7. Derailments, collisions and breakdowns were not uncommon in the early days of steam and the anti-railway lobby warned travellers of the dangers of rail travel, which ranged from catching pneumonia to death through accident. Insurance companies offered to cover anyone who feared injury on a railway journey in 1871.
205 × 138 mm

GREAT WESTERN RAILWAY.

CHRISTMAS HOLIDAYS

1st and 2nd CLASS RETURN TICKETS

ISSUED ON

FRIDAY, 23RD DECEMBER,

And intervening Days, will be available until

SATURDAY, 31st DECEMBER, inclusive.

Third Class Return Tickets

WILL ALSO BE ISSUED BETWEEN

LONDON

(PADDINGTON, VICTORIA, BATTERSEA, CHELSEA, AND KENSINGTON STATIONS)

AND

EXETER, YEOVIL, WEYMOUTH

AND

DORCHESTER

On *FRIDAY*, the 23rd of *DECEMBER*

And intermediate days, available for Return up to and including

SATURDAY, 31ST DECEMBER.

FARES.		
TO OR FROM	s.	d.
Exeter and back	21	0
Weymouth „	18	0
Dorchester „	17	6
Yeovil „	15	0

Third Class Tickets will be available by Third Class Trains only.

10. Special fares over holidays were advertised on handbills like this one issued by the Great Western Railway for the Christmas period.
272 × 176 mm

8. The pasteboard railway ticket was created by Thomas Edmondson in 1837 and it brought some uniformity to the size and style of tickets. In this selection are tickets from the Bermuda Railway company, looking rather like a pre-war bus ticket; a scholar's ticket on the Uganda Railway, a first class ticket from Shellalieh to Luxor in Egypt, a sleeping car ticket from Khartoum, a seat registration ticket for a journey to Cornwall, a return ticket from Bushmills to Portrush, a first class ticket from Priok to Kemajoran and a plain London and South Western Railway ticket from Waterloo to Putney.
58 × 30 mm

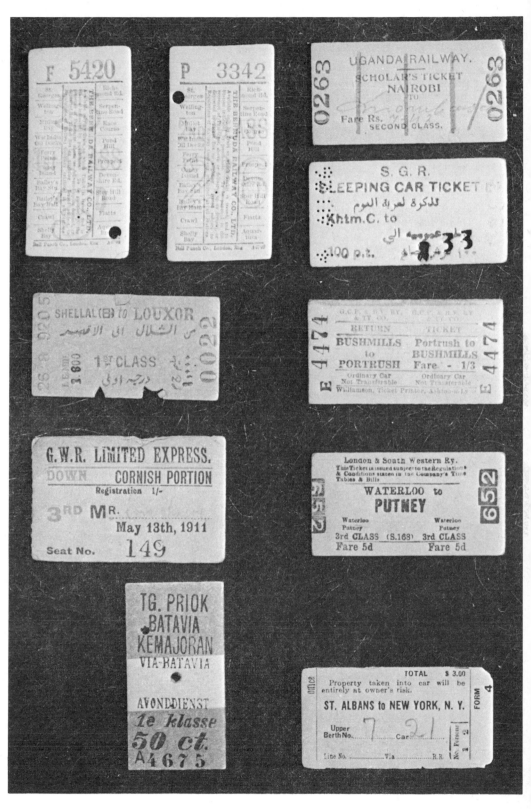

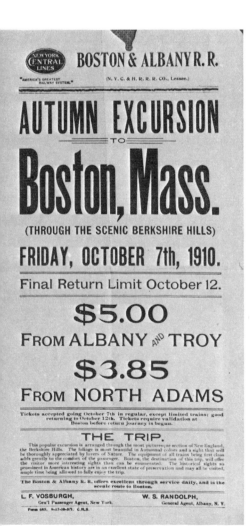

11. The railway excursion system was universal and helped to increase traffic. This one was for an autumn excursion in Massachusetts in 1910.

16. The hotel business was a natural development for the railway companies who built large establishments at their main termini. The Euston Hotel and the neo-gothic palace at St. Pancras served northern visitors to London.

13. Map sales thrived after 1840 but it was difficult to find competent draughtsmen or indeed detailed Ordnance Survey maps on which to base the railway maps. The Midland Great Western Railway map describes the route from Dublin to Galway.   137 × 220 mm

15. Most railway systems published leaflets which described their services though these often omitted times of arrival and departure at stations en route. The Midland Railway claimed that it had the most picturesque route between Liverpool, Glasgow and London.
190 × 90 mm

16a. Railway menus became more colourful and depicted scenery en route. This one offered Mock Turtle Soup, Cod au Gratin & Beef Stew for lunch.
195 × 125 mm

17. The luggage label was an expendable item with a short life. Famous people often had their own labels printed. This one was printed for the Duke of Wellington's servant, whose duty it was to collect his lordships game hamper from the station.   75 × 160 mm

4. Wyld's map of the railways claimed to be sanctioned by the Board of Trade and cost one shilling.
0 × 160 mm

18. Freight was the main means of livelihood for the railways and manufacturers sent their goods to their wholesale customers via the railways who took on the job of distribution. In these invoices coal, boots, shoes and potatoes are the products transported.
255 × 137 mm 125 × 204 mm 140 × 184 mm

PULLEN, VIRGIL & CO.,
Express Forwarders,
And General Foreign and Domestic Agents.

MERCHANDISE AND PACKAGES
OF EVERY DESCRIPTION,
SPECIE, BANK NOTES, &C.,
Will be forwarded DAILY, in charge of Messengers to and from

MONTREAL, NEW-YORK, QUEBEC, TROY, BOSTON
AND ALL INTERMEDIATE PLACES.
NOTES, DRAFTS, & BILLS COLLECTED,
And Orders attended to with Promptness and at Reasonable Rates.

The attention of careful Messengers on the Passenger Trains, will be given to Receiving, Forwarding, and promptly delivering Goods, &c.

Goods, Packages, &c., Called for and Delivered in any City.

OUR TROY & BOSTON EXPRESS
Makes a perfect arrangement for forwarding or receiving Goods in the New England States, and the connection with other Express Companies, extending through the States of the Union to California, England and France, perfects the system of Express, by which business can be transacted at home or abroad, with great care and attention, and at most reasonable rates.

Debenture Goods or Goods in Bond, will receive the prompt attention of one of the partners, in New York, and be forwarded with all despatch. Invoices should be sent with all goods going to Canada. Passage tickets for the London, Liverpool and New-York Packets, and Drafts for any amount from £1 upward, payable at any Bank in England, Ireland, or Scotland, without Discount, for sale at the office in Troy.

OFFICES.—In New-York, 16 Wall Street, and 118 Centre Street; Troy, 221 River Street; Montreal, 183 St. Paul Street; Quebec, St. Andrew's Wharf; Boston, Fiske & Rice, Rail-Road Exchange.

J. A. Pullen,   E. H. Virgil,   E. L. Stone,   G. A. Darling,   E. T. Dudley.

N Y Oct 28 1853

Snyder Blackiston has delivered to us one Box Marked Wm Law Esq

Shusham

To be sent by us, as Forwarders only, to _____
to be forwarded thence to the place of destination, and we in no event to be liable beyond our route, as herein receipted; neither are we to be held liable for any loss or damage, except such as shall arise from GROSS NEGLIGENCE. N. B.—The different Railroad Corporations between New-York, Montreal and Quebec, are not liable for the loss of, or injury to, any packages, goods or property entrusted to us—Valued under $150, unless otherwise herein stated.

For PULLEN, VIRGIL & CO.
C L Taylor

Contents Unknown.

R. V. Wilson, Printer, 225 River St., Troy.

19. As the freight business grew it was handled by forwarders who took on the organisation and paperwork involved in the movement of goods.

41

20. Railway companies used to publish reports of the amount of freight movements every month; they also published newspapers which promoted the idea of using the railway as a freight carrier. *The Mail Train* 350 × 240 mm. *The Railway Times* 285 × 210 mm

21. The handbill taking sides in a dispute is a familiar item of early railway ephemera. This one, written by an 'anonymous' author sounds like an attempt by the railway to ensure that objections to a level crossing at Peterborough do not receive public support. 280 × 225 mm

22. The railways have always aroused controversy. In recent times there has been a struggle between those who believe that non-profitable lines should be scrapped and those who consider the railways a public service which should be maintained at public expense. This leaflet sought support for the retention of the Richmond–Broad Street line, which runs across North London, at a time when its closure was under consideration. 195 × 125 mm

CHAPTER 4

Public Road Transport

Until the nineteenth century, there were virtually only two ways in which the average citizen could get about the streets of his town—either on horseback or, for most people, on foot. Some cities offered short-stage coaches, and there were also hackney coaches, sedan chairs or, early in the nineteenth century, cabs. And the well-off had their private carriages. But that was about all.

Then came the omnibus—a coach 'for all', as the Latin word could be translated. The first such vehicles appeared on the streets of Paris in 1819, when Jacques Lafitte introduced an eighteen-seater. There they were seen by an English coachbuilder, George Shillibeer, and in 1829 he introduced his own clean and comfortable 'Shillibeers' to the citizens of London. His first versions of the omnibus could carry twenty-two passengers, were drawn by three horses, harnessed abreast, and offered a journey taking about an hour from Paddington to the Bank of England for one shilling, or sixpence for anyone boarding half-way along the route.

In a printed notice announcing his intention of running an omnibus 'upon the Parisian mode' Shillibeer gave specific starting hours; 9, 12, 3, 6 and 8 o'clock from Paddington Green to the Bank and 10, 1, 4, 7 and 9 o'clock for the return journeys. This document is unusually specific for its day. Travel and transport operators were on the whole disinclined to publish timings, but the 1830s saw the beginnings of the timetables as a universally accepted institution.

The early London omnibuses, being classified as short-stage coaches, could not legally stop in the streets to pick up and set down passengers, though they seem to have done so all the same, until the 1832 Stage Coach Act formally permitted the practice. By an Act of 1838, omnibuses had to display their Stamp Office licence number and a notice stating the maximum number of passengers allowed on board at any one time. Drivers and conductors also had to have licences and to wear number plates. The police licensed London omnibuses, and usually local councils licensed the omnibuses in their own towns. The paperwork of licensing forms a major portion of the ephemera of public transport.

Much of the success of Shillibeer's omnibuses was due to the fact that he began operations at a time when the climate of opinion was right for introducing public transport in towns. People were becoming conscious of the needs of city dwellers and workers for better transport, and the 1820s and 1830s saw many experiments with various kinds of public transport.

With steam shipping well under way, and the railway boom also forging ahead, it is not surprising that many people considered it a good idea to get steam to do the horses' work on the roads as well.

Sir Goldsworth Gurney had been experimenting with steam road traction in the mid-1820s, and it was a modified Gurney boiler and engine which powered Sir Charles Dance's steam-driven coach service, which ran for a few months between Gloucester and Cheltenham in 1831.

Perhaps the most successful of the steam carriage builders at this time was Walter Hancock. His *Infant* made several demonstration runs to Brighton and his *Enterprise*, running a service between Paddington and the Bank in London on sixteen successive days, was filled with eager passengers every time.

But steam traction faced many difficulties, including fuelling en route, the need to carry coke and water, the danger of boiler explosion and, above all, the hostility of landowners and turnpike trusts, all of which combined to bring these experiments with mechanical road transport to an end. By the middle of the century there was nothing left of these brave attempts but a few splendid old

1. Invitation to the official opening by King Edward VII of the Kingsway Subway in 1905. The subway was built to link the northern and southern lines of London County Council's tramway system, and began operating in 1906. 137 × 195 mm

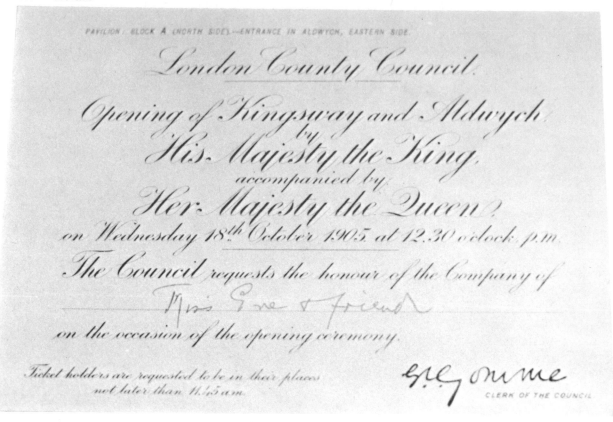

machines, some printed announcements of their runs, and a few pamphlets and popular prints. These, the ephemera of a truly transient phase, are rare indeed. While omnibuses and steam were being tried on roads in Europe, the Americans were experimenting with street railways, or tramways, as they were called, taking their name from the term used for the timber baulks of the very early railways. Baltimore had a street railway of a sort the year before Shillibeer's omnibuses appeared in London, and the New York and Harlem Line in Manhattan was operating in 1832. The vehicles used on the New York line were pulled by horses, as the city fathers were opposed to steam. Dubbed 'animal railways' (though no animal other than the horse appears to have been used to pull the carriages) these tramways soon became part of the environment in many American cities.

When the first permanent street tramway was eventually opened in Europe, in Paris in 1855, its name clearly indicated its origins: Chemin de Fer Américain.

The first public street tramway in England—as opposed to tracks which ran down piers—was opened in Portsmouth in 1865. By the 1870s, street tramways had been built in many English towns and cities and were also operating throughout Europe. Some of these were steam-driven, but the horse was not to be superseded until

electricity became a practical proposition in the 1890s. Then the horse's days were indeed numbered and by World War I, tramways, with few exceptions, were powered by electricity. Many American street tramway tickets of the electric age showed an illustration of the horseless vehicle itself.

Electricity also made possible a great leap forward in underground railway building, that other great nineteenth-century development in urban transport. A banquet (marked by a splendid invitation, and attended by the Prime Minister and other notables), signalled the opening in London of the world's first underground railway, the Metropolitan Railway in 1863. Its trains were steam-driven, with the locomotives designed to consume their own steam. The first deep-level 'tube' was also opened in London. This was the City and South London Line, opened in 1890, and was driven by electricity (rather than the cable traction originally planned for it), which had already proved successful in America on the Baltimore and Ohio system. The line is now part of London Transport's Northern Line.

In time, electricity was itself to be ousted from street transport by the motor bus in many parts of the world, although electric trams still play a big part in public transport in Eastern Europe and the Far East.

2. The Kingsway Subway route in operation in the 1930s. → Illustrated cover of an LCC tramways guide and map, issued to mark the re-opening of the subway in January 1931 after it had been enlarged to take double-decker trams. 225 × 142 mm

To private enterprise must go the credit for starting most public transport systems in Europe, America and the countries of the old British Empire. In many cases, local and national governments did not step into the picture or take over operations until well into the twentieth century.

In Britain, the first municipal authority to find itself a tramway operator, rather than an issuer of licences to private companies, was Huddersfield in 1883. The motor bus routes of London were begun and operated by private companies until the 1930s, though the London County Council operated the tramways.

In the beginning, not all London bus companies issued tickets. Indeed, in the days of the Shillibeers, it would have been difficult to do so, as passengers passed their fares up through the roof to the driver, who was too occupied with his reins and horses to be issuing tickets. Later, many omnibus conductors carried a wooden fare box into which passengers dropped their fares. Other companies provided their conductors with roll tickets. The London tramways used printed tickets from their introduction in the 1870s.

Ticket issuing became general with the introduction of the bell punch, or box punch. This was based on a ticket-vending machine which had been in use in America, and was first produced in England in 1878 by the Bell Punch

Company, which at one time was the biggest machine and ticket producer in the world. London buses used the company's equipment until 1953. Because there were few fare stages at the turn of the century, it was possible to operate a colour code system—white for penny tickets, blue for twopenny tickets, red for threepenny tickets, etc. The box punch (which the conductor could not open) had a numerator inside, so that a tally could be kept of the number of tickets issued during the course of a conductor's day. The machine also punched a hole in the ticket, and the 'confetti' which fell into the box was available for counting at the end of the day—so many white bits, so many blue bits—providing an accurate check on the conductor's takings.

In the heyday of the system, the Bell Punch Company, who also printed tickets, printed 14 million tickets a year for the largest bus company, the London General Omnibus Company, which later became London Passenger Transport. The London County Council printed their own tickets for the trams, but used the Bell Punch machines to issue them.

As the London transport network grew, this system could not cope, and the roll ticket was introduced. (London's Underground always used the same sort of tickets as the railways.)

Copies of this guide are obtainable, free, from
LONDON COUNTY COUNCIL TRAMWAYS
23, Belvedere Road, S.E. 1

3. A double-decker tram runs along the Embankment in this cover illustration on a 1930s LCC Trams guide map and timetable.
137 × 83 mm; unfolds to 410 × 327 mm

4. A London 'Tube Map' of Edwardian times, sponsored by the *Evening News* newspaper.
135 × 88 mm; unfolds to 500 × 610 mm

As the bus companies also eventually issued a wide variety of tickets, including through tickets (which could be used on the Underground as well as the buses), season tickets, excursion tickets, and children's tickets—ticket collecting alone provides the ephemera seeker with a wide field for exploration.

As the illustrations in this chapter show, there is also a splendid variety of illustrated papers to be found amongst the ephemera of public transport. Maps and timetables are obvious examples, as are posters and other notices.

Ornately printed invitations to the openings of lines, stations and subways attest to the value placed on the workings of the public transport systems, and children's games are a mark of their interest value. Behind-the-scenes operations also provide much of interest: company rules and regulations, operating instructions, the brochures of coach builders and ticket vending machine makers, early licences for bus drivers, returns of takings and passenger movements . . . the list is endless, and so is the ephemera.

6. A coronation souvenir from 1937: a Leicester City ticket for a tour of the decorated areas of the city.
45 × 95 mm

7. A special London Transport ticket aimed at helping the visitor to London. The ticket could be used on any branch of the London Transport network.
83 × 98 mm

9. A day 'Rover Ticket' issued jointly by British Rail, Southern Region, and Southern Vectis, the Isle of Wight transport company.
102 × 47 mm

8. A ticket from Jersey, Channel Islands, offering cheaper and easier travel for holiday visitors.
120 × 47 mm

12. The Pegasus symbol was used to convey the idea of speed on this booklet issued to the public c1930.

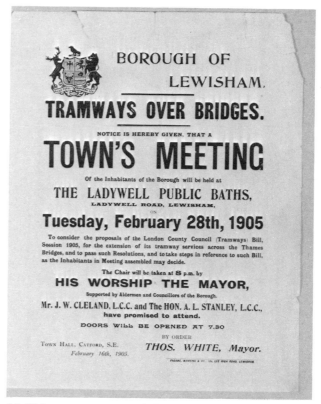

11. Reservation ticket for Gates' Omnibus Line in Binghamton, State of New York.
70 × 122 mm

10. This poster announced the intention to extend the Lewisham tramway services across the Thames.

16. Cover of a brochure put out by an American omnibus builder. The brochure illustrates the various kinds of carriage manufactured by the company noting the number of passengers carried and the various finishes available: 'Trimmed with black walnut, cushioned with plush or moquette' etc.
133 × 75 mm

13. Inter-city road transport in the 1940s: the timetable of Crosville Motor Services of Chester, whose conditions of booking allow small dogs on board, and whose London to Liverpool single fare was 25 shillings (£1.25).
190 × 127 mm

14. Cover of The Yorkshire Traction Company's tour programme for 1946.
212 × 140 mm

MARGATE RAILWAY
TO
LIGHTHOUSE **6d**
RETURN
Available on day of issue only.
DO NOT GIVE UP YOUR TICKET
AFTER IT HAS BEEN PUNCHED.

American Airlines
THIS BAG
DUE TO
TRANSFER
AT
ORD
ORIGINATING
FLIGHT
109
AA FORM OK19

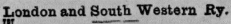

London and South Western Ry.
TO
Windsor

THE PROPRIETOR HOPES YOU
ENJOY THIS TOUR.
A
SIMILAR **TOUR**
WILL BE RUN ON
FRIDAY MORNING
WHICH GOES TO THE
**VILLAGE OF SKERABRAE AND
STANDING STONES OF STENNESS**
DO NOT MISS THIS VERY
INTERESTING TOUR

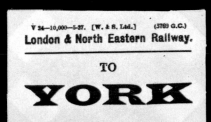

THURSDAY | FRIDAY | SATURDAY
LITTLEHAMPTON URBAN DISTRICT
COUNCIL.
FERRY TOLL 1d
Passengers are requested to see that this
Ticket is punched by the Collector when
purchased. Ticket to be shewn on demand.
SUN. | MON. | TUES. | WED.

Xh **2047**
London Transport Tramways
Ser 13 33 35
4d Work. (A)
Return journey only
Transfer Section

REED'S
Excursion Coach
To Ventnor.

Providence and Worcester Railroad.
WORCESTER.
W FIRST CLASS. **1**

London & North Eastern Railway.
TO
YORK

Cu **3100**
L.P.E.R.
1/- **ALL
DAY**
CANCEL HERE ONLY

GREAT WESTERN RAILWAY
No **202** Rate £ : :
FROM
TO
BETWEEN
WEYMOUTH &
THIS TICKET IS TO BE GIVEN UP ON EXPIRY

"VERMONT."
Captain WM. H. FLAGG.
1874.
Please have this Check ready at Landing.

L.N.E.R.
LUGGAGE **PE**
From
To
Via **PETERBOROUGH & L.M.S.**

33120
BRENTFORD MARKET
4d TOLL

Ak **0015**
BOURNEMOUTH—SWANAGE
Motor, Road & Ferry Co.
**BRIDGE
PASSEN-
GER**
MON.
TUES.
WED.
THUR.
FRI.
SAT.
SUN.
Available for one
journey over
Ferry only.
Not transferable

P. & A. CAMPBELL. Ltd
Landing Ticket
LUNDY ISLAND

No T 7481   No T 7481
EURAILPASS **1**ST CLASS
a CLASE
VALID **21** DAYS FIRST DAY
VALABLE JOURS PRIMERO DIA
VALEDERO DIAS
VALIDO DIAS LAST DAY
ULTIMO DIA
MR. JANE F. BABSON
Sr
Signature, Firma
Passport/Pasaporte N°

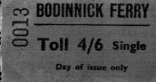

0013 **BODINNICK FERRY**
Toll 4/6 Single
Day of issue only

COWES FERRY
FLOATING BRIDGE
TOLL 1½P
For Person as per Schedule
Williamson, Ticket Printer, Ashton

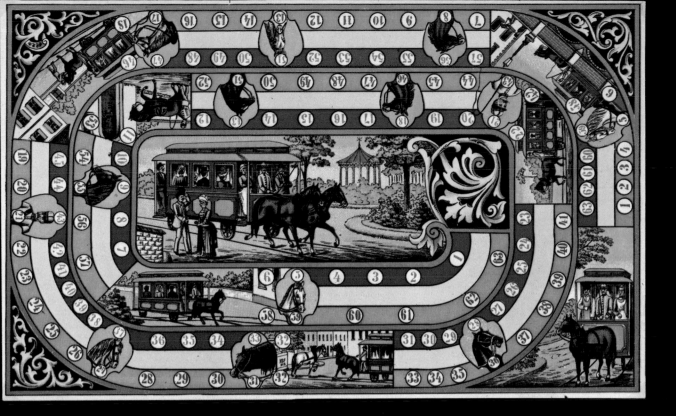

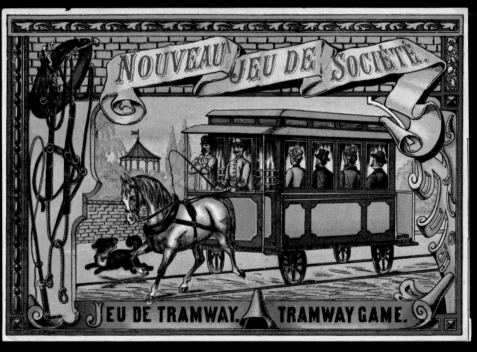

NOUVEAU JEU DE SOCIÉTÉ.

JEU DE TRAMWAY. TRAMWAY GAME.

30, RUE DROUOT, ET RUE DE FLANDRE, 3.
PARIS   Ancⁿᵉ MAISON BURNET.
ENTREPRISE GÉNÉRALE DE DÉMÉNAGEMENTS POUR PARIS & LA PROVINCE
BOUSSARD CHARLES, SUCCⁿ.
DÉMÉNAGEMENTS
VOIES DE TERRE & DE FER
Wagons capitonnés pour transport de
Mobiliers par Voies de terre et de fer

Kind hearts
can make
DECEMBER
blithe as
MAY

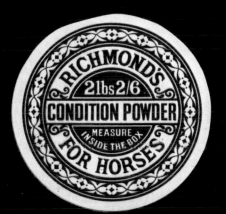

RICHMOND'S
2 lbs 2/6
CONDITION POWDER
MEASURE
INSIDE THE BOX
FOR HORSES

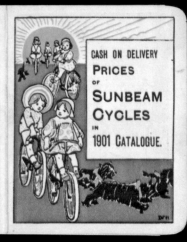
ALL
ORDERS
FOR
STANDARD
PATTERNS
DELIVERED
FROM STOCK.

CASH ON DELIVERY
PRICES
OF
SUNBEAM
CYCLES
IN
1901 CATALOGUE.

To Attain Perfection in
BICYCLE RIDING,
AND AVOID ACCIDENTS,
GO TO THE
NORTH LONDON BICYCLE SCHOOL.
P.T.O.

Chicorée
La SANS RIVALE
Chez tous les épiciers

BACON'S
CYCLING
&
MOTORING
ROAD
MAP
WITH
ROUTE GUIDE
ENGLAND
AND
WALES
Sheet 5
In Cloth Case - - - 1s. net.
On Cloth, in Case, 1s. 6d. net.
London: G. W. Bacon & Co., Ltd., 127, Strand.

THE MACHINES WHICH SELL AT SIGHT.

Bouillon
Cibils

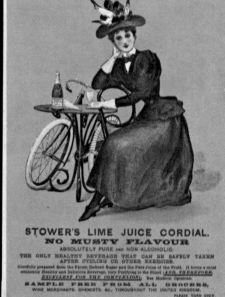
STOWER'S LIME JUICE CORDIAL.
NO MUSTY FLAVOUR
ABSOLUTELY PURE AND NON-ALCOHOLIC.
THE ONLY HEALTHY BEVERAGE THAT CAN BE SAFELY TAKEN
AFTER CYCLING OR OTHER EXERCISE.
SAMPLE FREE FROM ALL GROCERS,
WINE MERCHANTS, CHEMISTS, &c., THROUGHOUT THE UNITED KINGDOM.
PLEASE TURN OVER.

AM HAVING A LOVELY TIME HERE

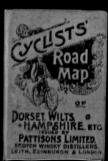
CYCLISTS'
Road
Map
OF
DORSET, WILTS
& HAMPSHIRE, ETC.
ISSUED BY
PATTISONS LIMITED,
SCOTCH WHISKY DISTILLERS,
LEITH, EDINBURGH & LONDON.

CONSTRICTOR
NEVER
TYRES

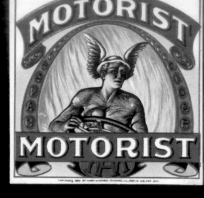

Shell Road Map
MASSACHUSETTS • CONNECTICUT
RHODE ISLAND

SHELL

SPECIAL SHEET. POPULAR EDITION.

ORDNANCE SURVEY

DISTRICT MAP

G R

LONDON
(NORTH)

Scale : 1 Inch to 1 Mile

Price : Three Shillings

WAKEFIELD

RETAIL CATALOGUE
1. 9. 32

Castrol

MOTOR OIL

THE
AUTOMOBILE ASSOCIATION
TOURING MAP of
ENGLAND & WALES
TWELVE MILES TO AN INCH
*Issued exclusively to Members
by the Automobile Association
Fanum House, New Coventry St, London W1.*
PUBLISHED BY
JOHN BARTHOLOMEW & SON. L*TD*
The Geographical Institute, EDINBURGH

RICHFIELD
STRIP
MAPS

HANDY REFERENCE
MAPS OF
CALIFORNIA
OREGON
WASHINGTON

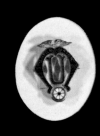

BACON'S
NEW HALF-INCH MAPS
CYCLING
AND
MOTORING
LONDON
DISTRICT
SHOWING DANGER HILLS

PRICE
1/ NET

ON CLOTH
2/ NET

LONDON :
G. W. BACON & CO., L*td*., 127, STRAND.
WITH INDEX

MANCHESTER
GUARDIAN
AND
EVENING NEWS

MOTOR ROUTES

We have just arrived here.

SOUTHBOURNE

THE Island & the MANX ELECTRIC RAILWAY AT A GLANCE.

On August 25th, 1902, Their Majesties the KING & QUEEN travelled over this Line

SNAEFELL SUMMIT HOTEL

Ramsey

The Royal Mail and Popular Route to Ramsey.

Health-Giving Trips!
Sea & Mountain Breezes!

A Continuous Panorama of Charming
Coast, Mountain &
Woodland Scenery.

Cars from DERBY CASTLE
every few minutes.

FIRST-CLASS REFRESHMENTS
AT ALL POINTS.

Laxey

Derby Castle STATION

Douglas

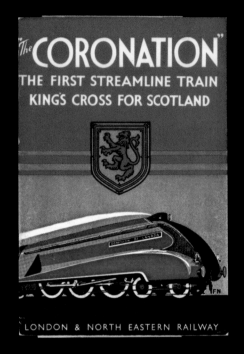

"CORONATION"
THE FIRST STREAMLINE TRAIN
KING'S CROSS FOR SCOTLAND

LONDON & NORTH EASTERN RAILWAY

Connecticut Valley Electric Transit Route

"Take the Trolley"

LOOK OUT FOR **Soapine.**

KENDALL MFG CO

PROVIDENCE, R.I.

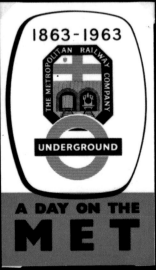

1863 - 1963

THE METROPOLITAN RAILWAY COMPANY

UNDERGROUND

A DAY ON THE
M E T

KENT & EAST SUSSEX RAILWAY
EGGS
WITH CARE

LONDON'S TRAMWAYS

**TRAVEL QUICKLY
READ IN COMFORT**

THIS COMPARTMENT
IS NOT TO BE USED.

EVERYTHING IS FIRST CLASS
AT CLEVEDON.

FIRST

THE OVERLAND

S. S. PIERCE CO.

OVERLAND

JUST ARRIVED.

At DARTMOUTH.

CHEMINS DE FER DE MONTAGNE

Chemin de fer à vapeur du Brocken (Harz).

VÉRITABLE EXTRAIT DE VIANDE LIEBIG.

ORANGE-EMPIRE TROLLEY TRIP

Through California's Orange Kingdom Operates Wednesdays and Sundays 9:AM.

PACIFIC ELECTRIC RAILWAY

LOS ANGELES · CALIFORNIA

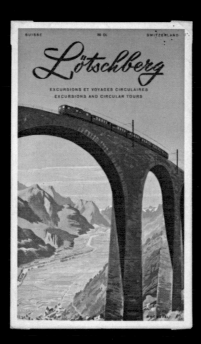

SUISSE · 90 Ct · SWITZERLAND

Lötschberg

EXCURSIONS ET VOYAGES CIRCULAIRES

EXCURSIONS AND CIRCULAR TOURS

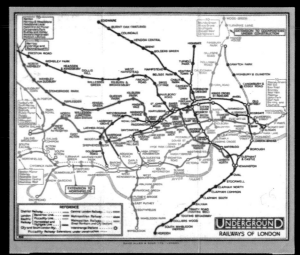

UNDERGROUND RAILWAYS OF LONDON

"LOOK HERE, UPON THIS PICTURE." "AND ON THIS." Shakespeare

ORDINARY PETROLEUM OIL

STRANGE'S A-1 CRYSTAL OIL

SEVERN VALLEY RAILWAY SANTA SPECIAL

BIRN BROTHERS LONDON

The penny sheets of Mammoth Scraps published by Birn Brothers 27 Finsbury Street London are the most liked and the best selling

BOURNEMOUTH CENTENARY FETES.
:: JULY 6—16, 1910. ::
HOTEL METROPOLE, BOURNEMOUTH.

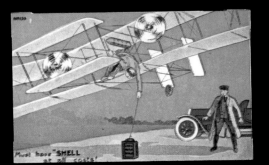

THE AEROPLANE.

ACTION SONG for Schools
Curwen's Edition, No. 1364.

WORDS AND MUSIC BY

THOMAS FACER.

LONDON
J. CURWEN & SONS LTD.
24 BERNERS St. W.

Price One Shilling.

Copyright U.S.A. 1909 by J. Curwen & Sons Ltd.

INTERNATIONAL AVIATION MEETING

BOURNEMOUTH 1910
JULY 6-16
SOUTHBOURNE AERODROME

PROOF ONLY.

IMPERIAL AIRWAYS

about Flying to and from
SWITZERLAND

Soapine
RISES ABOVE
EVERYTHING

A SAFE TRIP

GOOD BYE

L' Areostatica

VERO ESTRATTO
DI CARNE LIEBIG

MARCH, 1904. SIX COMPLETE STORIES and RIDER HAGGARD'S Serial, "THE BRETHREN: A ROMANCE OF THE CRUSADES." Price 6d.

CASSELL'S MAGAZINE

EDITED BY
MAX PEMBERTON

CASSELL & COMPANY, Limited: London, Paris, New York & Melbourne.
Published Monthly. Subscription Price, 9s. 6d. per Annum, post free. [All Rights Reserved.]

Guide to the
Airport of London
(Croydon).

AIR MINISTRY. PRICE **2**d.

OXO

BAXTER'S
IMPERIAL STOUT
THIS LABEL IS ISSUED ONLY BY BAXTERS (NORTHALLERTON) LD BREWERS THORNTON-LE-MOOR
TRADE MARK
REGISTERED

OUR USA **BIRD**

HUNTLEY & PALMERS
BISCUITS

5 - The start.

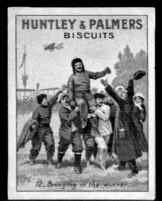

HUNTLEY & PALMERS
BISCUITS

12 - Bringing in the winner

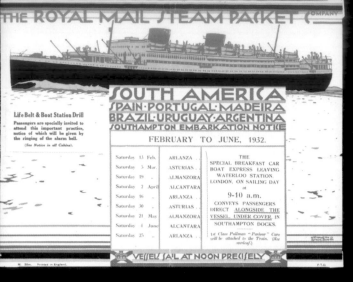

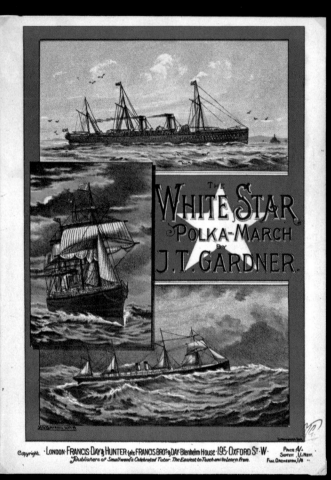

P & O
(Conveying His Majesty's Mails)
PASSENGER SERVICES
EGYPT INDIA CHINA JAPAN AUSTRALASIA

FREQUENT & REGULAR SAILINGS
TO AND FROM
LONDON, MARSEILLES AND BRINDISI
RETURN TICKETS AVAILABLE FOR TWO YEARS
AT A FARE & A HALF TO & FROM PORTS EAST OF SUEZ
ROUND-THE-WORLD-TOURS YACHTING CRUISES

OFFICES 122 Leadenhall Street E.C.
Northumberland Avenue W.C. **LONDON**

WHERE TO STAY

PUBLISHED BY THE GORDON HOTELS, LIMITED.

Telegraphic Address, "CUNARD"
CUNARD LINE
FROM **NEW YORK** OR **BOSTON** TO **LIVERPOOL**

CUNARD SPECIAL at RIVERSIDE STATION, LIVERPOOL.
3 Hours, 50 Minutes, from LONDON.

"LUCANIA" Alongside LIVERPOOL LANDING STAGE.
Passengers embarking

1900 · JANUARY · 1900

SUN		7	14	21	28
MON	1	8	15	22	29
TUE	2	9	16	23	30
WED	3	10	17	24	31
THU	4	11	18	25	
FRI	5	12	19	26	
SAT	6	13	20	27	

SAILING DAYS IN RED

Also Regular Sailings to HAVRE, ITALY, the ADRIATIC, and LEVANT.

Sailings from
NEW YORK OR **BOSTON**
ON TUESDAYS, THURSDAYS, & SATURDAYS, calling at **QUEENSTOWN**

Agent :

Across the Atlantic in 5½ days.

NEW YORK:
29, Broadway.
BOSTON: CHICAGO:
99, State Street. 67, Dearborn Street.
GLASGOW:
Nn. Jamaica Street.
MANCHESTER:
18, Brazennose St., Albert Square.
QUEENSTOWN:
Cunard Wharf.
HAVRE: PARIS:
23, Quai d'Orleans. 38, Avenue de l'Opera.
LONDON:
13, Pall Mall, & 51, Bishopsgate St.
LIVERPOOL:
8, Water St., and 1, Rumford St.

EMPRESS STEAMERS
A Merry Christmas & a Happy New Year

HOLIDAY TOURS

SEASON **1900**
Organised and arranged by
THOS. COOK & SON *London E.C.*
Ludgate Circus, **LONDON** E.C.

HOTEL
BÄREN
BERN

INTERLAKEN

HOTEL
METROPOLE

EXCURSIONISTS
MAY SECURE

£100 FOR THEIR **FAMILIES**
IN CASE OF
DEATH BY RAILWAY ACCIDENT,
IN A TRIP OF ANY LENGTH,
With an allowance for themselves when Hurt of £1, 0s. 0d. per Week
for a period not exceeding Six Months,
BY TAKING

AN INSURANCE
TICKET, COSTING **TWO PENCE.**
Premium to Insure £500 in a First-Class Carriage of Excursion
Train, or £3 per Week for Injury—SIXPENCE.

N.B.—For Insurance Tickets, ask the Clerk to whom you Pay
your Railway Fare.

66 CORNHILL. WM. J. VIAN, Secretary.
[Two Ons.

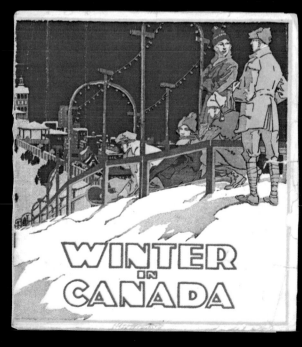

WINTER IN CANADA

HÔTEL
QUIRINAL
ROME

BRUFANI PALACE HÔTEL PERUGIA

SCRIBE *Hôtel* **PARIS**

THE CARAVAN
SAFETY MATCH · MADE IN SWEDEN

THE STEAMER
PARAFFIN MATCHES
MADE IN SWEDEN

QUEENIE SAFETY MATCH
STEAMSHIPS TRADING Cº LTD.
PAPUA
MADE IN SWEDEN

CICLISTA
TRADE MARK
MADE IN SWEDEN
JULIO BALETTE

THE ROWING
SAFETY MATCHES
MANUFACTURED IN SWEDEN.

THE ROWING
SAFETY MATCHES
MANUFACTURED IN SWEDEN.

THE VICTORY
SAFETY MATCHES
AVERAGE CONTENTS 60 MATCHES PR BOX.
MADE IN SWEDEN

EL AEROPLANO
STA ANA Y SONSONATE
MADE IN SWEDEN
FABRICADO EN SUECIA
REPUBLICA EL SALVADOR
FOSFOROS DE SEGURIDAD

E. CHEMBEE
BICYCLE DEALER
AND
REPAIRER.
BUCKINGHAM ST. PENANG

WHEEL
SAFETY MATCHES
W. I. M. Cº LTD.
MADE IN INDIA

THE TUG SHIP
SAFETY MATCH
MADE IN SWEDEN

THE TORPEDO
MADE IN SWEDEN
SAFETY MATCH

CAVALIER und DAME
MATCHES MADE IN SWEDEN

VELO
MATCHES
UDDEVALLA
MADE IN SWEDEN

PROTECTION FROM FIRE
DAMP PROOF
TRADE MARK
SAFETY MATCHES
MANUFACTURED IN SWEDEN

BALLOONS
MADE AT JÖNKÖPINGS WESTRA
SWEDEN
SAFETY MATCH

GIVE YOUR
LETTERS WINGS

Use
AIR
MAIL

WE ARE
EXHIBITING AT
The IITH INTERNATIONAL
MOTOR
EXHIBITION
OLYMPIA
ORGANISED BY THE
SOCIETY OF MOTOR
MANUFACTURERS
AND TRADERS LTD
NOV. 8·16.

INTERLAKEN.

GRAND HOTEL VICTORIA.

OFFICIAL PASS

Name

MILITARY AEROPLANE COMPETITION, 1912

RAILWAY
BENEVOLENT
INSTITUTION

Great Western Railway

LONDON (Paddington)
AND
LEAMINGTON SPA
(In 1 Hr. 30 Mins.)
BIRMINGHAM
(In 2 Hours.)
Wolverhampton
(In 2 Hrs. 25 Mins.)

RESTAURANT CARS

September 26th. 1927,
and until further notice.

Felix J. C. Pole   General Manager.

No. 48. Martin Billing, Son. & Co., B'ham.

A. G.
GREIFENHAGENER KREISBAHNEN
DIRECTION
GREIFENHAGEN

THE ROYAL AERO CLUB
MEMBERSHIP CARD
1915
OF THE UNITED KINGDOM

HANSEATISCHE SEEVERSICHERUNGS GESELLSCHAFT
F.P.
1901
HAMBURG

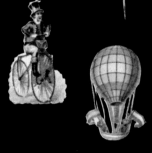

Brock's
Crystal Palace
Fire-work
Balloons

STARGARD-CÜSTRINER EISENBAHN-GESELLSCHAFT
DIRECTION
CÜSTRIN

HEINRICH KUTZNER BAUUNTERNEHMER
CHARLOTTENBURG

STAHLBAHNWERKE FREUDENSTEIN & CO.
CÖLN A/RH.

SEDAN.

DAMPFSCHIFFAHRTSGESELLSCHAFT F.d. NIEDER u. MITTELRHEIN
DÜSSELDORF

CHAPTER 5

Everyone's Transport

With the bicycle and the motor car, we come to our own personal transport. We no longer have to depend on Mr. Shillibeer's omnibus, or the London Steam Tramway Company's timetable or even Sir Freddie Laker's Skytrain. The transport sits in our own shed, garage or backyard; it is for us to pump up the tyres, fill up with fuel, and get going.

Cycling caught the popular imagination in the mid-nineteenth century. Before that, those extraordinary celeripedes, draisiennes, dandy-horses, boneshakers and velocipedes had been very much the province of daring young men and mechanically-minded readers of the popular scientific magazines of the day. But by the late 1860s, the velocipede had become sufficiently cheap to buy and convenient to ride to appeal to the ordinary man. The word 'bicycle' took over from 'velocipede' as the correct nomenclature for the two-wheeled velocipede which had been largely developed in France and America. The first cycle races were run in France and Britain, the first cycling clubs were founded, and the earliest cycling magazines were published.

One of the most sought-after of all pieces of cycling ephemera is a song-cover dating from 1869: *The Great-Wheel-Hoss-I-Pede*, as sung by W. F. Collins of the Christy Minstrels. 1869 was also the year of the first known motor-cycle, a velocipede to which a single-cylinder steam-engine unit was fitted.

Bicycle production went ahead at speed, and soon bicycles, tricycles, ordinarys (penny-farthings), safety bicycles and sociables were all in production. By the 1880s, many famous names were already well-established, including Humber, Rudge, Hillman, Raleigh and Ariel, and by the end of the decade Dunlop had improved the pneumatic tyre to the stage where it was being fitted to racing bikes and winning races.

Advertising, as well as selling the bicycles themselves, played a big part in promoting the idea of cycling as a socially desirable activity. Much of the best advertising was to be found in magazines and trade journals, but manufacturers' trade cards, catalogues and leaflets were also printed with typical Victorian exuberance and more often than not were illustrated with line drawings of machines, making them splendid reference material.

Their wording makes them of value to social historians. Imagine, for instance, the pictures conjured by advertisements for 'bicycle schools', extending to riders the opportunity to 'learn accomplishments' and 'attain perfection', or for 'Practice Rooms' at cycle shops where buyers might be instructed in the use of their machines before venturing out into the streets on them.

Because cycling became such a popular activity, advertisers were given a golden opportunity to advertise other products by attaching them to its coat tails. Hence the plethora of soap and biscuit wrappers, cordial and embrocation labels, match boxes, post cards and valentine cards, all illustrated with cycling themes. The appeal was two-way: the soaps and biscuits, cordials and embrocations were better, it was implied, because they were used, eaten or drunk by cyclists; on the other hand, if you bought these products yourself, you would become a better cyclist.

More practical ways of becoming a better cyclist were outlined in the many cheap pocket books devoted to cycling which began to pour forth from publishers in the 1870s. These little books on the theory and practice of bicycle riding often carried imaginatively illustrated covers and editorial line drawings, making them particularly attractive collectors' items.

Other booklets to develop from the cycling boom included pocket diaries, in which cyclists could record their daily mileage, journey times and bed-and-breakfast places, and maps folded into sizes suitable for pocket or knapsack.

Not every cyclist wanted to emulate men like the Land's End-to-John O'Groats record breakers. Improving on G. P. Mills' 1886 time of 5 days, 1 hour and 40 minutes on an 'ordinary' would take a major effort, but the thought of miles of quiet open roads lured more and more cyclists away on two-wheeled holidays. This was a fact not lost on map printers and publishers, who in Britain were quick to produce a wide variety of suitable maps, mostly based on the Ordnance Survey, the 25-inch series of which by the 1880s covered the whole of England and Wales.

Sadly for the cyclists of the '80s and '90s, who shared the quiet roads with a few farm and carrier waggons, the petrol engine was to catch up with them all too soon, filling the roads with cars and motor cycles. The first motor cars were appearing on public roads by 1889, and Henry Ford's cheap assembly-line Model T of 1908 and W. R. Morris's Morris-Oxford of 1912 pointed the way to the car-owning boom of the 1920s.

In 1912, Morris' garage in Oxford still called itself the 'Morris Cycle Works' and advertised 'Cycle and Motor Repairs', but after the 1914–18 War, the emphasis changed, and the bicycle took second place. On both sides of the Atlantic, bicycle manufacturers turned to making cars, and figures for car ownership soared. Private car owners in the United States increased three-fold in the 1920s; in Britain they quadrupled, and the sales of motor cycles also boomed.

In Britain, no car owner was legally permitted to drive at more than 20 miles an hour throughout the 1920s, nor did anyone have to pass a test to obtain a driving licence until 1935, though everyone had been obliged since the 1903 Motor Car Act to hold a driving licence.

Today, the driving licence, road tax disc and car log book are just three of thousands of pieces of ephemera with which the collector may depict the motoring scene. Motor ephemera conveys the impact of the petrol engine on everyone's daily life, reflecting changes more radical than anything the ordinary man had experienced in former times.

Collections of Edwardian-period ephemera of the motor car must almost certainly include advertisements and leaflets for special motoring clothes, chauffeurs' liveries and the like. A collection from the 1920s however, when the 'car of the people' had become a reality, would include popular cigarette-card collections and road maps with covers showing ordinary families out for a spin— wholly ignoring the predelictions of the rich.

Certain types of motoring ephemera are common to all periods—illustrated brochures for scores of makes of cars; repair bills and invoices, often with illustrated letterheads; receipts for petrol; membership cards for automobile clubs and organisations (it was the Automobile Association which set up the first petrol station in England in 1920); entry tickets to car racing events; the trade cards of motor salesmen, car hire companies, taxi and cab operators, motor mechanics, accessory shops. . .

These are merely the ephemera of businesses directly connected with the car. Let the net spread wider to include advertising in which the motor car is used as an image in selling other merchandise, and ephemera multiplies a hundredfold. In the early 1900s, scarcely a product from chocolates to cigars, from children's games to greeting cards does not hitch its presentation to the concept of the horseless carriage.

5. Advertisement for special riding, cycling and other corsets from the High Wycombe Advertiser, 1896.
145 × 255mm

2. In this ambiguous advertisement, which appeared on the back of Cycling Echo in 1896, Dunlop appear to be implying that they would also be willing to repair any puncture the balloon might have. 245 × 185mm

"What a Glorious 'Xmas Present!"

RUDGE WHITWORTH, Cycle Manufacturers, COVENTRY, BIRMINGHAM, & LONDON.

1. An advertisement for the Rudge–Whitworth ladies' bicycle, c1895.
240 × 158 mm

3. Elegant type, attractive scroll work and plenty of illustration characterise this biscuit advertisement from the 1890s.
248 × 200 mm

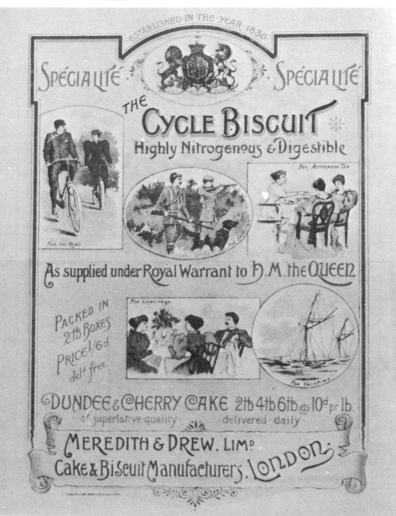

4. Into the future with a bicycle: the simple yet effective cover of a 1935 Sunbeam booklet.
213 × 176 mm

12. A small poster, c1930, for a popular make of cycle light battery. →
380 × 254 mm

11. Entry form card for a challenge cup cycle race in 1898.
74 × 112 mm

ESSEX CYCLING UNION, Ltd.

Reopening of High Beech Track, May 7th, 1898.

ENTRY FORM FOR "KING'S OAK" CHALLENGE CUP RACE (10 Miles Unpaced).

To E. W. BENWELL, 4, Osbaldeston Road, Upper Clapton, N.E.

Please enter Mr.....................of......................

License No............as the Representative of the.....................C.C. in the

above Race. Mr.....................of......................License No............

is Reserve man.

Both the above have been First-Claim Members of the above Club since March 1st.

I enclose entry fee, 2/-

Signed.....................

.....................Address.

.....................Club.

7. Front cover of a fold-up road map for cyclists, 1895–1900.
170 × 98 mm

10. This 1937 American Youth Hostels membership card emphasises cycling.
124 × 78 mm

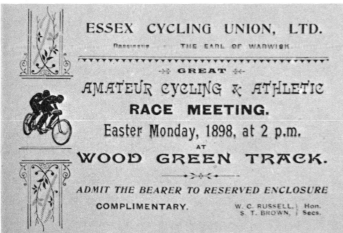

9. A variety of types and decorative borders make an eye-catching layout for this cycle race meeting entry ticket, 1898.
125 × 200 mm

8. A 1907 pocket diary with contents specially devised for cyclists.
128 × 80 mm

69

13. An elegantly designed advertisement for 'a very
gem of British engineering'—the Reynold
motor cycle chain.
315 × 230 mm

14. Receipted invoice from a Suffolk car and cycle repairer, 1929.
170 × 204 mm

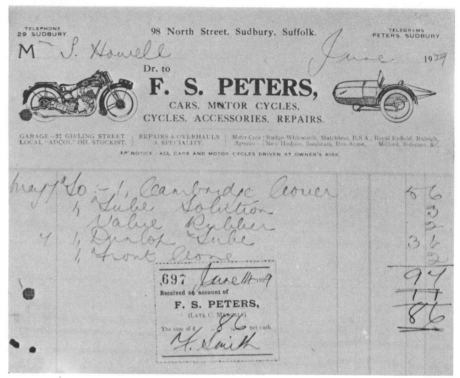

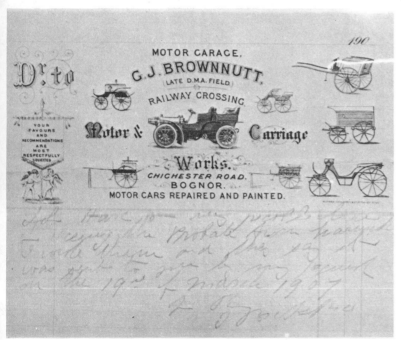

15. A splendidly ornate bill head from 1907.
172 × 205 mm

16. This letterhead is as much of interest for its contents as for the
illustration. The writer anxiously enquires about her brother, a
passenger on the British liner, the *Lusitania*, which was torpedoed
on 7 May 1915.
272 × 208 mm

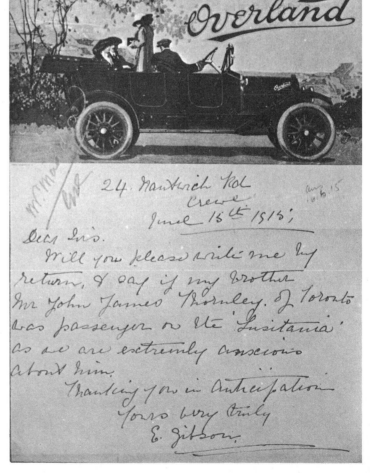

19. An English billhead of 1912.
260 × 205 mm

18. The *Motor Car Polka*: songs sheets like this are always desirable collectors' items.
358 × 216 mm

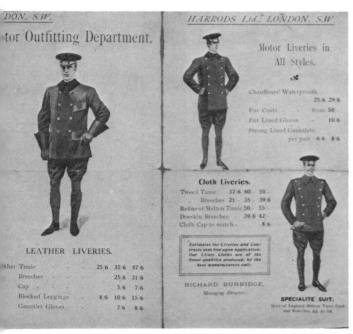

17. What the well-dressed chauffeur was wearing, c1910. These pages are from a Harrods catalogue.
181 × 217 mm

20. Edwardian Sunlight soap magazine insert; an effective picture, simpler in style than Victorian Sunlight advertising.
157 × 114 mm

21. The treatment of this otherwise elegant advertisement suggests that President Poincaré travelled standing in his car's doorway.
302 × 210 mm

23. A third hand on the steering wheel: an English advertising leaflet.
122 × 182 mm

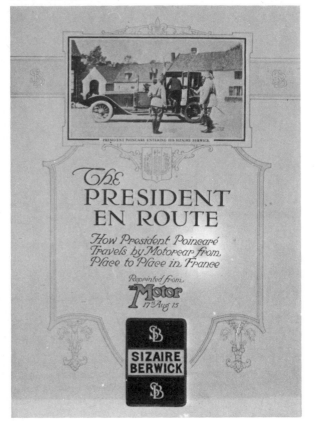

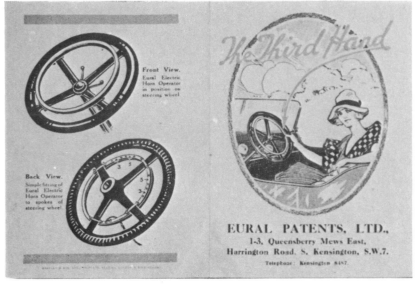

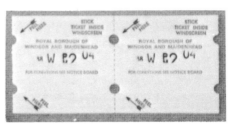

26. A petty irritation of modern motoring—a car-park windscreen sticker. The type first appeared in the 1970s and was issued from a coin-in-the-slot machine.
29 × 63 mm

22. American car salesman's trade card.
101 × 216 mm

25. A folding road map aimed at motorists and cyclists, published by the *Daily Herald* newspaper in 1953.
220 × 124 mm

ROLLS-ROYCE LIMITED

have for disposal a few new

25/30 H.P. Rolls-Royce

Cars of the pre-Wraith type

at specially attractive prices

Rolls-Royce Ltd
14-15 Conduit Street London W.1
Mayfair 6201

24. Car hire price list, c1912.
278 × 168 mm

27. Getting rid of old stock, Rolls-Royce style.
200 × 160 mm

CHAPTER 6

AIRBORNE

After the Montgolfier brothers had taken to the air in a balloon in 1783, and every print shop in Paris was selling engravings of their exploit, the public woke up to the possibility of flying. This interest, like flights in space in our own day, was soon exploited by purveyors of entertainment. Resorts, vying with each other to amuse the customers arriving on excursion trains, were quick to feature balloon flights. Their attraction continued throughout the century as we see in a 1890 handbill for a Bank Holiday (1). Jules Verne wrote *Six Weeks in a Balloon* and a balloon flight featured in his most famous book, *Around the World in Eighty Days*.

Balloon flying was only a prelude to flying in heavier-than-air machines and when Orville and Wilbur Wright proved that this was possible in 1903, public interest in flying reached fever pitch. Even before the Wrights' official flight, the Aero Club of Great Britain had held its first meeting in 1901. At its first international meeting in 1909, Henry Farman performed the incredible feat of flying over 100 miles. At about this time air meetings were taking place everywhere, especially at seaside resorts which provided natural landing strips on the sand. In Bournemouth, in 1910, a special programme was printed for the Centenary Fêtes which included an international amateur flying meeting.

A scheduled passenger service began in Florida in 1914, but the Great War prevented the inauguration of regular commercial passenger flights in Britain. Here, the first flights began in 1919 after the government had lifted the restriction on them. The first air brochure was produced in 1920 by Thomas Cook (2) who used converted Handley Page bombers for pleasure trips.

The immediate commercial future for aviation lay with mail-carrying services and the first attempt to establish an air mail in Britain was in Blackpool, from where Claude Graham took off with a bag of letters for Southport. Unfortunately he did not reach his destination.

Despite minor setbacks, air mail and freight services developed quickly, spreading all over the world as air passenger services were established. The first successful air mail service in India was from Allahabad to Naini Junction and the first service between Britain and India was introduced in the 1930s (3). The cost of air mail was high and the GPO set about persuading the public that it was worth paying for. The forward-looking image of the new services was publicised widely on the cover of the GPO magazine (4). This made an association between the two most modern means of transportation, showing a smart van together with an 'H class' airliner.

As with the introduction of new methods of transport in the previous century, there was a rush to speculate in an industry which seemed to offer the opportunity to make quick profits. The cost of starting a new air service was great, however, as we see from the share certificate of the Compagnie Générale Aeropostale, whose capital was twenty million francs (5).

The high cost of flying (an Air Union ticket for a single trip to Paris is marked 1000 francs) (6) deterred all but the rich from indulging in air trips. Those who could afford it were given a level of personal service unknown today. Passengers were chauffeur-driven to London's airport, then at Cricklewood, and escorted to their free-standing wicker armchairs in the aircraft where during the flight

20. Fantasy has always accompanied invention. This 'atmospheric→ machine' was intended for the transport of troops and government despatches. A promotional broadside published by the inventor in 1843.   500 × 380 mm

Entered at Stationers' Hall.

Pirates will be Prosecuted.

THE GREAT AERIAL NAVIGATOR, OR ATMOSPHERIC MACHINE!

Under the superintendence of the "Aerial Conveyance Company," for the conveying of Passengers, Troops, and Government Despatches to India and China, in the short space of Five Days, by means of a new and improved system of "AERIAL NAVIGATION" Adapted also to proceed on Water or Land, and can be used as a most destructive instrument of War; likewise for scientific and astronomical purposes: altogether forming in the wonderful adaptation of its various complicated parts, its mechanical combinations and mighty developement of power, one of the most extraordinary inventions of modern times.

Description.

This gigantic production of the genius of man, will assuredly become the greatest of all mechanical wonders, when its mighty powers for good and for evil are hereafter developed.

Aerial locomotion, on the old balloon principle has had its allotted time for exciting the wonder and admiration of the curious; but like stage coaches, balloons will soon be numbered among the things that were, as Atmospheric Machines of the above description are gradually adopted; in reality, annihilating both time and space, and by a more rapid intercommunication destroy the prejudices of nationality, and thus conduce to moral happiness.

No 1. Is the main body, or chief support of the whole apparatus; the only part which at all resembles the balloon principle. It is in the form of a heart, composed of 26,000 yds of finely woved and prepared silk, doubled throughout, somewhat in the form of a small balloon, enclosed within a larger one. It is to contain 160,000 feet of a newly discovered gas, formed by a secret chemical combination, considerably lighter than Coal Gas; while a fresh supply can always be kept up for the purpose of inflation, and thus obviate one of the greatest difficulties attendant upon the old system, both as regards power and security.

Around the internal part of the exterior covering is placed a *framework*, connected with another of smaller dimensions, but separate about two feet, resting upon the outside of the interior part which encloses the gas, composed of the strongest and best tempered steel, with whalebone wicker work, having slides and curiously formed joints, so that the whole machine can be drawn together, and closely packed up after it has descended, and the gas evaporated.

& 4. Are *Parachutes*, so placed that when the main body of the machine is inflated, and ascends into the required current of air; they assist the power of suspension, and contribute to a more steady balance of the whole; thus entirely preventing the violent occillations that oftentimes occurred with the old balloons, and caused a very unpleasant sensation to be felt by novices in aerial locomotion. They can also be made to open and shut by means of their connection with the internal framework, and thus, by forcing on an average about 500lbs. weight of air each upon the main body, they consequently assist the machine in descending.

. A *Telegraph*, situated on a small dome in the centre, at the top. It is composed of the same material as the interior frame work, of which it forms a part; and it has cross pieces so arranged as to serve the purpose of steps, by means of which ascension to, and descension from the telegraph can be easily effected. When within fifty miles of any place during clear weather, at a low elevation, or from 100 to 200 miles at higher and proportionably well situated elevations, various signals can be made to others at a distance, in the space of a few minutes, which is effected by working the two upright arms, and altering their positions as occasion may require. By those means persons can state their business and whatever they wish concerning the despatches, goods, and passengers they are conveying.

. Is a *valve*, for conveying off the steam, when generated too quickly; it is raised by means of a double line at the back, and when required to be lowered other lines are attached to the fore part for that purpose. The steam is generated by quick lime and other chemical processes united. The valve is entirely of a new construction, containing within the pipe, and situated about the middle, a curiously constructed cylinder, and the top entirely opens when the cover is drawn up.

6. Another pipe, connected with the engine and chemical furnace, in the lower part of the machine, for carrying off the smoke and superfluous particles.

. and 8. Are revolving *Fan-wheels*, connected with the internal frame before mentioned, and moved by the engine below, which so act as to fan the air with great force, and thus propel the machine forward. There are two others on the opposite side, for the like purpose. The fans are made of strong canvas, and revolve on the spokes; and their power of acting upon the atmosphere is equal to any of the larger kind of windmills.

Is another *Fan* of much greater power, in the form of the tail of a bird, which opens and shuts together, and moves up and down in the same manner, worked by the engine before stated, and is situated at the *Stern* of the machine.

10. Shows an *Observatory*, with a most beautiful and very powerful Telescope, on the same principle as Sir John Herschell's grand instrument at the Cape of Good Hope. The mode of ascent and descent is by an enclosed staircase very curiously constructed. Like the gentleman here observed to be looking through the Telescope all lovers of science can enjoy themselves with greater pleasure than can be experienced on the earth.

11. At the base of the Observatory is the form of an eagle, the wings of which also act like fans, moved by machinery. On its head is a weather-cock, and out of its mouth is issuing smoke, which comes through a pipe placed in the interior, from the same place as mentioned in No. 6. This part forms the *Stem, or forepart* of the machine.

12. This is the upper part of the *Carriage* suspended to the main body of the machine, the same as a Car is usually attached to a balloon. It is called the *Day Chamber*, for the convenience and comfort of passengers in the daytime, when they want to enjoy the pure air and fine weather. It can also be used as a *Promenade* being sufficiently spacious for moderate exercise. Its dimensions are 24 feet long, by twelve feet wide, and 10 feet in height. It has a waterproof India rubber roof fixed in a mahogany frame, with handsome curtains which can be drawn together if required; supported by four beautiful veneered pillars, and surrounded by a strong ballustrade, erected breast high, the whole fixed together in the most secure manner.

In the floor is a well-staircase, by which passengers can descend to what is called the *"Night Chamber,"* which is compact, warm, and perfectly secured from the weather. It has a door in the centre on one side, and windows at each end on both sides of the chamber. It is of the same length as the upper chamber, but six feet wider and eight feet higher. Situate therein, enclosed within a fire-proof screen, is an *engine*, small in dimensions, but mighty in power, which moves the whole framework secreted in the internal part above and below, with every joint and member of its complicated machinery kept in constant and harmonious motion. Its Fans, Paddles, Wheels, Arms, Wings, and Tail, all working together—thus manifesting the ability of *man* to make every element of nature subservient to his purpose. At each end there are two private rooms, for either sex, so that every convenience that is possible in so small a space is adopted. One is the "Ladies' Department," and the other the "Gentlemen's," each room having chairs for six persons, a table, sofa, and all the small etceteras. The doors and partitions are made to take out, when the whole can be formed into a barrack for soldiers.

13. Is a boat, made (like the chambers above) after the Chinese fashion. It has a space of 6 feet on the deck, with bulwarks 3 feet high all round. Underneath, is a spacious hold, 9 feet in depth, for merchandise, naval or military stores, &c. There is a proof magazine for gunpowder, places for shot and shell, with 22 patent swivel guns, half of that number being placed on each side. Across the breech of each gun, over the touch-holes, is placed a *metallic rod*, one end of which is attached to a *Galvanic Battery*, and each gun is so constructed, that when the battery is charged, in a second of time a rapid succession of awful explosions will follow from the mouth of each piece of ordnance—pouring down their destructive fire almost perpendicular upon those *unfortunates* whoever might be exposed to it. In proportion, as the gas is expelled from the balloon part, it becomes filled with atmospheric air, and when it has descended by the other processes adopted for that purpose, if over the sea, or any navigable river, the boat can be made to float like vessels in the water, when the once gigantic *silk dome* above can be compactly folded up and then there appears sailing along a sort of *steam house*, to the "astonishment of the natives." Or, when it descends on land, then, the paddles can be drawn up, and the wheels can be used instead; when, behold! it now appears transformed into a steam carriage. "This is truly the age of wonders."

14, 15, 16, 17, 18, 19, 20, 21. Are *Fans, or Paddles*, the arms of which are moved by the *engine* before mentioned. They are constructed of india rubber, of an oval form, and hollow between the two sides, which are drawn tight on whalebone frames, with three air funnels on the sides and end of each of them, all composed of the same material which catch the air and adds to the force of their motions. They act as Fans on the atmosphere, and as Paddles in the water. This concludes our description of the external part of this "Great Aerial Navigator," and, there is nothing remaining to state respecting its internal arrangements excepting that the force of the engine, machinery, and chemical action on the whole, is equal to 200 horse power; also, it is calculated, that with 50 adult passengers, and when loaded with the amount of goods and other things it is required to carry, with the actual weight of the whole combined, it will not fall far short of 130 tons.

Incredible as it may appear to those ignorant of physical science, there is actually a *subtile and invisible agent*, known only to practical chemists, but first combined by the *Inventor*; which will suspend in the air even 20 times the above weight if used in proportion. With such means adopted for causing *Suspension*, also *Propulsion*, and *Repulsion*, by rising or falling into the required curent of air; and the principles of this machine brought into proper action, the public shall in a few months witness the glorious reality.

LETTER TO THE BOARD OF ORDNANCE.

London, Feb. 20th, 1843.

MOST NOBLE LORDS, AND HONORABLE SIRS,

As it is your especial duty to superintend the offensive and defensive operations of Her Majesty's land forces; and as all inventions for acquiring superiority in the art of war, must become, when proved to be practicable, a subject of the greatest importance, especially to England; therefore, be it known unto you, that I have completed after many years study, that, which I flatter myself, you will pronounce to be, one of the most extraordinary inventions of modern times, an Engraving of which, with a description, I here beg leave to lay before you.

A company of scientific gentlemen, the most experienced in the art of locomotion, has been formed for carrying into effect, that, which will ere long *prove a reality*, exhalt "fallen man," and elevate the whole human race in the scale of society. The unavoidable evils that will result by this invention clashing with other interests will only be of short duration, and will be compensated for, (nationally speaking) by the immense advantages that will accrue to England as the first of maritime countries, and the most universal of empires. That such will be the ultimate result, you will acknowledge when you have seriously read the above *description*.

I remain, yours respectfully,

The Inventor.

TO HER MAJESTY'S MINISTERS.

London, Feb. 22nd. 1843.

MY LORDS AND GENTLEMEN,

Placed at the head of a great nation, I call on you to avail yourselves of my *invention*, which I will prove to you, if adopted, all the nations of the earth combined can never stand against our power. But, my Lords, I do not mention that fact, with the view of making my country the tyrant of the world, but for the more noble purpose of causing her to be the arbiter of every good. With that view I penned my former letters and my late one to the *"Board of Ordnance."* I am about to apply to Parliament for a "Bill" or "Act of Incorporation," in order that I might legalise a company of gentlemen associated with me, for the purpose of conveying passengers, goods, despatches, &c. by means of my *"Aerial Navigator,"* either through the air, on water or land. Hoping that I may depend on your support, I will conclude by laying before you the accompanying *Description*, of an invention which I justly feel proud of, conscious, that if rightly used, it will redound to the honour and glory of my native country, and the welfare of the whole civilized world.

I remain,

My Lords and Gentlemen,

Your Obedient Servant,

The Inventor.

VICKERS, Publisher, 28, Holywell Street, Strand; and supplied by W. Brittain, 11, Paternoster Row; Allen, Warwick Lane; Cleave, Shoe Lane; Turkess, Wardour Street; Clements, Pulteney Street; and if ordered, by all other Booksellers in Town or Country.

Letters (post-paid) attended to by E. HANCOCK, at J. Cook's, Printer, 1, Corner of Sadler's Buildings, Fann Street, Goswell Street.

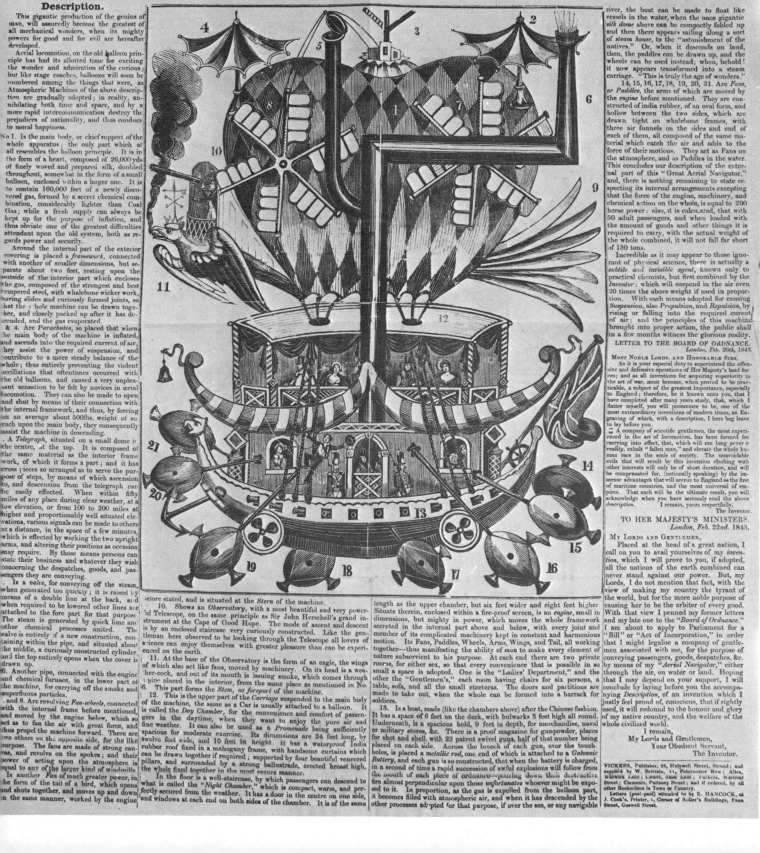

they were served a menu including hors d'oeuvres, lobster, chicken and other delicacies, and appropriate drinks.

Flying was an elitist indulgence, a mode of travel for the rich and the famous. But those who could not afford it could play at it. Board games featuring air travel became popular. 'Concours d'Aviation' (7) was played in France and for British would-be air travellers there was 'Aerial Post' (8). The Aero Club (later the Royal Aero Club) arranged races to promote the air industry, including the Aerial Derby round London in 1923 (9). Postcards featured aircraft—though these were equivocal as to whether it was more thrilling to be airborne or to be safe on the beach with an attractive young lady. The idea of flying also caught on at fairgrounds, where simulated flights were more exciting than the scenic-railway (10).

The promotion of air travel became more intense as the business developed, and pioneers like Charles Lindbergh, Amy Johnson, Jim Mollison, Amelia Earhart, Wiley Post and other heroes risked their lives in exploring new sky routes. Watching aircraft taking off and landing at the airports became a new pastime and at London's Croydon airport a guide book was available.

Inevitably the romance of flying inspired a desire to learn the art of flight and flying schools sprang up all over the world with offers of joy trips for modest sums, and flight lessons for a little more. The Beatty School of Flying (12) operated out of Hendon airport, where air displays also took place. An annual event was the Royal Air Force Display, a programme of which, dated 1932, shows the rapid advance in aircraft design since the Beatty School days.

After World War II, flying for everyman became a reality because of the development of the jet engine. Jets replaced the old propeller aircraft on schedule services and made them available for charter flights. Competition between airlines led to intensified publicity to persuade the public to use specific air services. Posters like the one produced by Air France (14) sought to impress the name of the airline on the public mind. The image of flying became sleeker, projecting the luxury that was now available to everyone.

However, the comfort of the first commercial flights, with meals served at tables between the seats and ample leg space, was rapidly disappearing as it became necessary to increase the seating capacity of each aircraft. In an effort to impress the identity of the airline on the public, air companies employed designers to create an image specific to the airline. The livery of the aircraft itself, the uniforms of the crew and the hostesses, and every piece of ephemeral literature carried the new corporate identities.

As hotels had done in the past, the airlines created special baggage labels, like the Varig one (16), to advertise the fact that the passenger had flown on that particular airline. Embarkation cards like the Allegheny Airlines item (17) also carried the company name.

Pilots aroused everyone's admiration and became the heroes of Hollywood movies, as well as the inspiration for a spate of popular songs. Typical was 'Airman, Airman, don't put the wind up me!' (15).

Among the items that the passenger was showered with in an effort to engage his or her loyalty, were souvenir booklets of the flight (18), magazines and disposable slippers, eyeshades etc. All of these carried the airline identity, as did the safety regulation instructions tucked in the pocket of every seat.

For the ephemera collector who seeks the unusual, air travel provides themes unlikely to be repeated in the future of aviation. One of these is the era of the hydrogen airship, which ended with the disasters of the R101 and the *Hindenburg*. Zeppelins proved an exceptionally luxurious form of air travel, offering spacious lounges, bars and cabins, and they seemed at one time to provide the answer to the problem of long-distance travel. The *Graf Zeppelin*, most successful of the airships, made 144 crossings of the Atlantic and the Deutsche Zeppelin Reederei published a book giving details of its construction (19).

Another aircraft that created unusual ephemera, for those lucky enough to find it, was the flying boat. Like the zeppelin, the flying boat was one of the answers to the question of long-distance flying. The British developed the 'Imperial' flying boats for routes to Africa and the Far East, and the United States introduced the famous 'Clipper' flying boats of Pan American Airways.

Since the development of jet aircraft and the evolution and control of the industry through bodies like the International Air Transport Association, a certain uniformity has crept into the business of flying and therefore into its ephemera. But the future seems to offer more scope, with prospects of greater competition—and even the remote possibility of flights on the space shuttle.

2. The first international air service was from Hounslow to Le Bourget in 1919, using a converted De Havilland 4A bomber. The Handley Pages on which Thomas Cook passengers flew were 12-seaters and flew from London to Paris.
200 × 155 mm

4. Airmails created a new source of revenue for the GPO and they promoted them energetically. The idea that it was smart to write by airmail is evident in the style of this cover photo. 243 × 180 mm

3. Many foreign airlines were subsidised by their governments but British and American airlines kept themselves going by carrying mail and freight. Air mails made a significant contribution to communication across the vast expanses of North America and the even greater distances between the outposts of the British Empire.
125 × 157 mm

1. The daring young men of the nineteenth century who rode off the ends of piers on bicycles, dived into tiny tanks of water or made parachute drops were usually given the courtesy title of Professor. In this case Professor Clark is accompanied on his ascent (but not on his descent) by Captain Jackson, described as a daring and experienced Midland Aeronaut—the only English balloonist to allow a parachute descent from his craft.

5. Some early air services were set up by impecunious ex-World War I pilots, but many of them were unable to remain in a business which had high running costs. The Compagnie Générale Aeropostale had a 2 million-franc capital base.
318 × 326mm

6. The 1920s air fare to Paris was about £20 single. George Holt Thomas of Air Transport thought a fare of £5 could be profitable with a 75 per cent load, but passengers were not forthcoming and his company went out of business in 1920.
138 × 104mm

8. Aerial post was an airmail game. The early days of the real thing were more hazardous. The picture shows the cover of this board game, c1920.
125 × 557mm

12. The Beatty Flying School advertisement appeared in *The Aeroplane*, 1915. The copy suggests that the flying school was a way into the Services—the only place where flying jobs were available in any number.

13. The Royal Air Force, formed from the Royal Flying Corps, gave exhibitions of flying in order to encourage recruits.
246 × 154mm

19. Public curiosity about how zeppelins worked was satisfied by this booklet, published by the German Zeppelin Line in the 1930s.

14. An attractive Air France poster, c1930, which sold the idea of travelling by air not only by depicting the aircraft but by projecting the idea of effortless travel to sophisticated places.

18. In the mid 1920s flight souvenir booklets proved that one had actually flown, investing their owners with the same aura of importance as million-mile certificates presented by modern airlines to regular travellers.
196 × 115mm

15. *Airman, Airman, Don't Put the Wind up Me,* a comedy song reflecting the public's nervousness at the prospect of flight.
310 × 243mm

16. Only a few years ago luggage labels like the Varig and Aeroflot items gave the person to whose luggage they were attached a certain distinction. In the 1980s, with air travel in some places as commonplace as motoring, they have disappeared.
62 × 118mm

7. Concours d'Aviation was a game about air races. The imaginative cover shows daring young men in their extraordinary flying machines over Monte Carlo.

11. Aerial war stories captured the public imagination largely due to the real-life war exploits of pilots like Richthofen, the 'Red Baron', and Bishop. *Une Campagne en Hydravion* is a French war story about the air war at sea.
195 × 137mm

10. Those who could not afford to go up in the real thing got a thrill out of flying machines at the fairground—like this one at the Italian Exhibition at Earl's Court in 1904.
87 × 140mm

17. Boarding passes identify the passenger who has presented his ticket and documentation to the authorities. Today most of them are purely functional and similar from airline to airline.
215 × 92mm

CHAPTER 7

AT SEA

Before the age of steam, a journey by sea was an arduous experience that attracted few people other than those whose ambition drove them to seek their fortune through trade, the prizes of war, or piracy. All these activities were of an essentially individual nature; and on the whole, they yield little in the way of printed paper for the modern collector. There were, of course, the various bills relating to the carriage of goods by sea and there were the licences to trade and even to operate as a privateer (1a), but since the running of a ship was entirely the responsibility of its master, there was little need for the voluminous documentation that became an obligation once the increase of sea-going traffic made it necessary to regulate its passage.

Even when the rules of sea-going began to be laid down, the master retained his unique authority and his responsibility for ensuring that the ship sailed safely and profitably. The master had total control over his crew and the choice of passengers who sailed with him. These, like the traders who shipped their goods on his ship, would be attracted by his personal reputation and his own discreet publicity. This was often in the form of a card which announced to the public the name of the captain, his ship and destination and the services he was offering (2).

The age of steam and iron screw-driven ships brought to an end the world of the individualistic sea captain and introduced the era of steamship companies, whose affairs were carried on according to strict business principles and who found themselves subject more and more to maritime laws regulating every aspect of life at sea.

The more structured development of maritime activity began to produce the printed matter that is collected by today's ephemerist. The ephemera includes shipbuilders contracts, certificates of registration, crew lists, port clearance papers and of course passenger booking forms, tickets and all the other items of printed paper that were necessary for the business of passenger shipping.

As standards of shipboard comfort improved there also began to appear printed menus and wine lists (3), reflecting the increasing luxury of life at sea.

Ships had always carried passengers, but never in large numbers or as an organised business until the screw-driven steamships made their appearance in the middle of the nineteenth century. The paddle steamers which had attempted to set up regular transatlantic trips were never really successful and the most ambitious and largest of them all, Isambard Kingdom Brunel's *Great Eastern* ended her life cable-laying across the Atlantic.

It was Samuel Cunard who first made a success of regular steamship sailings. Cunard was a thoroughly practical man and his fleet made no attempt to rival the glorious failures of Brunel, nor indeed the ships of his American competitor, Edward Knight Collins. Collins' ships were bigger, more luxurious than Cunard's but they were unable to pay their way. Another competitor was William Inman who made a success of his shipping line by carrying emigrants from Europe to America.

At that time, and for many decades afterwards, America was a land of promise for millions of Europeans and Inman realised that they would be prepared to pay to go on his ships as long as he could keep the fare low. He therefore quoted an emigrant fare of £3.50 to New York and £4 to Canada. His intention was to take 1000 emigrants on each trip, but by now the authorities were beginning to regulate the conditions under which ships could ply their trade. Inman therefore reduced his intended capacity but still made a profit.

Emigrants to the New World were the business that kept steamships in profit for many years and the shipping

1. From the earliest days of commercial shipping it was obligatory for ships to announce their departure from port. This certificate was issued for the *Carnatic*.
100 × 159mm

1a. The holders of shares in the armed ship *Yorktown* hoped to profit from her prizes.   125 × 202mm

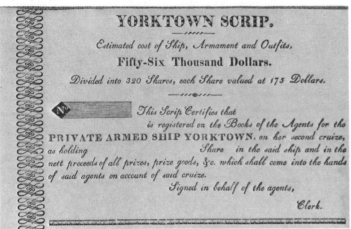

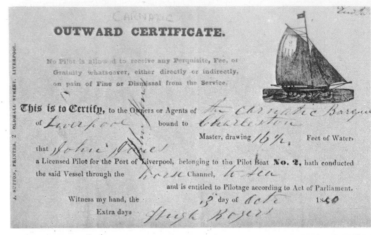

5. Emigrants were offered inducements to start a new life in the colonies. In this handbill families are offered free passage for their children and loans with which to buy livestock, while household workers are guaranteed jobs.
260 × 205mm

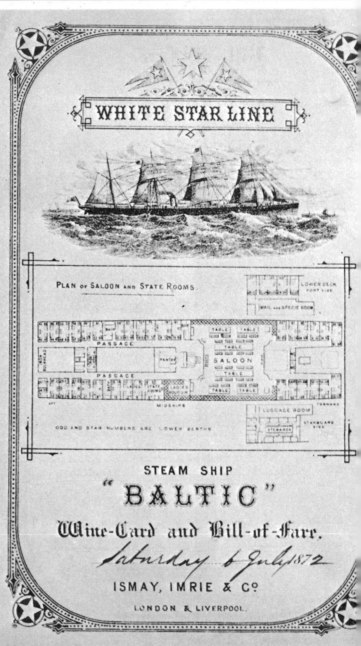

3. The wine card and bill of fare of the White Star ship *Baltic* showed a picture of the ship and its deck plan.
211 × 132mm

companies promoted this traffic with widespread newspaper advertising and handbills (5). Some of these even offered such incentives as free tracts of land—included in the fare.

The development of shipping to the East was as important as the service across the Atlantic, especially after the opening of the Suez Canal in 1869. This opened up the steamship routes to the British Empire of the East, where there was already a good business in carrying military and Civil Service personnel. In addition, Australasian emigration, and the discovery of gold in New Zealand and Australia helped to increase the flow of traffic.

The 1890s saw the beginning of international rivalry across the Atlantic with the British, French, Germans and Americans building bigger, faster and more luxurious ships. In 1890, the Cunard Line was advertising passages from $60 to New York and offering steerage accommodation at very low rates. A ticket for the *Umbria*, which still carried sail, cost £20.00 in 1890 to New York and promised the passenger twenty cubic feet for his luggage and victuals for a First Class passenger (4). Twenty years later, the tonnage of the ships had risen from 8,000 to 32,000 on such famous ships as the *Mauretania* and the ill-fated *Lusitania* (sunk by a German torpedo in World War I). With the *Titanic*, another doomed ship, these were among the most luxurious ships afloat before World War I and they compellingly expressed the confidence and affluence of British society at the time.

People who travelled first class on the transatlantic liners were at the top of the social tree. They included the rich and the famous and when Hollywood launched its stars on the world they too travelled in style on the liners, enhancing their glamour. As in luxury hotels, top people liked to know who else was on the ship in first class and the passenger list (7), used by White Star as early as 1870 (8), became more elaborate. (Really important people often attempted to travel incognito, however.)

Travellers like these came from a class that was used to servants and they expected the same attention while travelling as they received at home. Steamship lines made a point of pampering their passengers and as labour was cheap they were able to employ large crews to do just that. The service continued on shore, with social staff to meet passengers on arrival at ports of call or final destinations. The Cunard Line even kept a special staff in Paris to look after passengers who had travelled on their ships, making them known to passengers by means of a card showing their photographs (9).

Of course, those who travelled on the great liners were pleased to let the world know about it and the steamship lines exploited human vanity by printing attractive labels to advertise themselves, as did hotels (and, later, airlines) (10a).

The most glamorous of all forms of sea travel, the cruise, generates ephemera of a specially romantic nature. This type of sea voyage enabled the steamship companies to keep ships busy between major voyages promoting the notion of sea travel as an escapist world where everything is perfect. The first cruises were to Scandinavia, the Midnight Sun Cruise becoming a perennial favourite, and to the Canary Islands and Madeira. Later came the Mediterranean cruise (11) and then world cruises.

The glamour of the sea was reflected in ephemera far beyond the practical documentation and promotion of sea travel and it was used in general advertising to suggest the excitement and appeal of faraway places. The label for 'Deep Blue Sea' apples (14) gives the fruit a romantic appeal that the ordinary home-grown Granny Smith could hardly hope to emulate.

A constant reminder of the glamour and thrills of travel was the wall calendar sent out by shipping companies to their customers. The Cunard specimen (shown in the colour section) illustrates every stage of the journey and still arouses nostalgia for the great days of sea travel. This same romantic appeal appears in the advertisement for 'Johnny Walker', where the whisky is associated with the whole glamorous history of sea travel.

Has the greater part of her dead weight on board, and will sail with all possible dispatch, direct for

SINGAPORE,

THE FINE NEW SHIP

FAVORITE,

Burthen per Register, 300 Tons, A 1 and Coppered.

WILLIAM COBB, COMMANDER.

Lying in the London Dock.

THIS VESSEL HAS EXCELLENT ACCOMMODATION FOR PASSENGERS.

For Freight or Passage apply to the COMMANDER on Board, at the Jerusalem Coffee House and Lloyd's; or to

JOHN PIRIE & Co.

3, Freeman's Court Cornhill.

Ellis, Printer, Old Broad-st.

2. Commander Cobb announces by means of this card that he is sailing for Singapore on a new ship the *Favorite*.
74 × 112 mm

7. The Lloyd Royal Hollandais Line was one of the competitors on the Atlantic run and its passenger list cover gave the impression of the speed and luxury of its ships.
199 × 127 mm

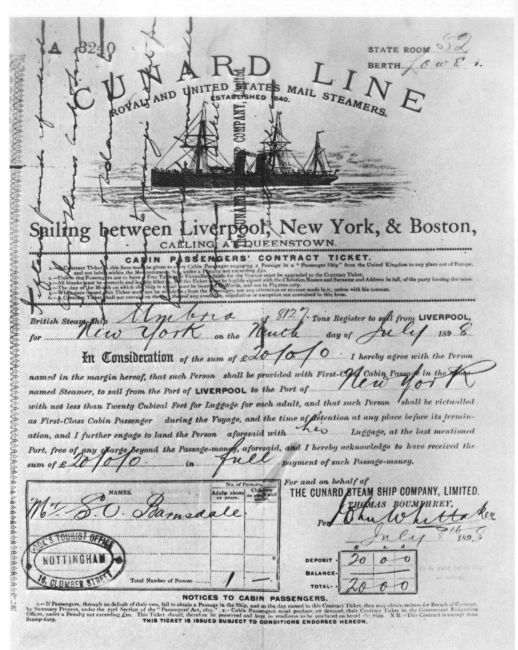

4. Regular passengers were provided with an imposing contract which gave the name of the ship and the price of the passage, in this case £20, from Liverpool to New York, first class.

9. It was essential that the illusions of perfection of life aboard should not be shattered by the more mundane reality of the trains that took passengers from the ports to the capital cities so the steamship companies put on special staff to make the transition easy.
88 × 125 mm

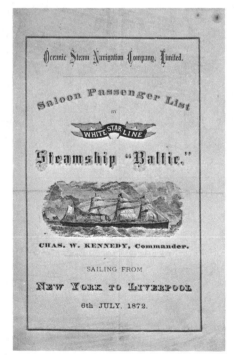

8. Passenger lists have been in existence a long time and like the newspapers at seaside resorts provided passengers with a means of checking up on their fellow passengers.

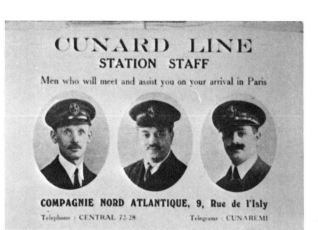

6. In the years before World War I steamship companies advertised their ships in the way→ that holiday companies do their hotels today. This Cunard Line advertisement shows the 32,000 ton *Lusitania*, designed so that she could be used as an armed cruiser in case of war. She continued to be used as a passenger ship and was sunk in 1915 with the loss of more than two thirds of her 1600 passengers.

10. Life on board, especially in first class, demanded a large wardrobe. There were as many as five changes of dress every day. Stateroom luggage was specially labelled and the rest of the necessities for a long stay in Europe were marked 'Not Wanted on Voyage'.
117 × 180mm

10a. Luggage labels like this one gave passengers a special cachet.
91 × 145mm

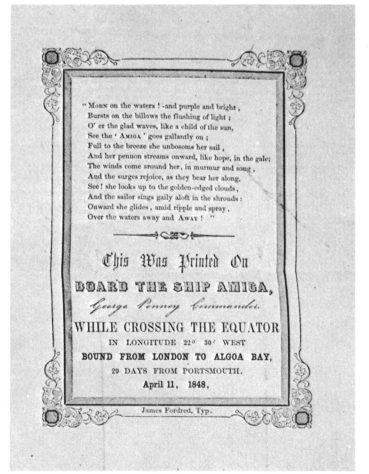

13. The Equatorial crossing was marked by a visit from Father Neptune, who shaved passengers and ducked them in the pool. The victims received a certificate in compensation.
225 × 179mm

14. Exporters and importers reminded their customers of the part played by shipping in international trade.
224 × 265 mm

11. Between the wars, cruises vied with the Alps as locations for romantic love. This 1935 folder, with its image of moonlit nights, well-dressed passengers and modern setting reflects the world Noël Coward sang about.
214 × 127 mm

It makes me proud to think I've seen
The paddle-boat become the "Queen".
Like Clyde-built ships, I've grown in fame –
The skill behind me's still the same.

15. The romance of the age of sea travel lasted until the very last of the big ships. In this advertisement Johnnie Walker associates the year of his birth with the first steam-driven paddle boats—and his continuing popularity with the launch of the *Queen Elizabeth*.
210 × 310 mm

The modern holidaymaker, clutching his wallet full of air tickets, hotel coupons, passport, transfer voucher, travellers cheques, insurance certificate and all the other documentation required for even a simple trip to a nearby country, takes it all for granted. In his lifetime paper has become an accessory of all kinds of travel and, though sometimes a nuisance, it is a universally accepted proof of entitlement.

With the right piece of paper one is assured of a seat in an aircraft or train, a berth on a ship, a bed in an hotel. In the event of the place to which the paper refers being unavailable, the paper functions as evidence of a promise unfulfilled, and ensures that a claim for compensation will be met. It was not always so. In the early days of leisure travel it was every man for himself. The eighteenth-century youth may have been accompanied by a tutor to steer him safely through the rapids of a European journey, but there was no guarantee that he would find a boat to take him over the Channel or an inn to shelter him. Nor could he demand a specific standard of accommodation or be certain that the landlord would not rob him during the night.

The lucky few had their own coaches and villas at the spas and resorts of England and the Continent, or their friends had; the rest had to make their arrangements as best they could. They would have to hire a coach which could involve them in paying the coachman as well as the coachman's food and overnight accommodation. This much we glean from a standard contract dated Rome, 9 April, 1851. The form, filled in by the contractor, gives details of his conditions of hire (1).

Early ephemera of holiday travel of this kind is rare and more likely to be found in the country of origin than abroad. Notices of the coach routes which traversed Europe and which were more frequently the mode of transport of the leisure traveller are more easily found, if only because there were more of them, especially on the Grand Tour routes through Germany, France, Italy and Switzerland. Both the latter countries are included in the announcement of a new 'diligenza' which travelled from 'Milano to Coira' (Milan to Chur in eastern Switzerland) (3).

Rattling and bouncing along unpaved roads, occupants of the coach had other worries beside the discomfort of the journey, for there was always the possibility that bandits might hold them up, or that they might find themselves passing through a cholera-infected area. (It is well known, though possibly apocryphal, that Lord Brougham while on his way to Nice learned that cholera had broken out there and therefore decided to stay at a small fishing village called Cannes, which, as the result of his lordship's presence, blossomed into a fashionable resort.)

Health certificates were often a requirement in those early days of continental travel. Sometimes these were necessary even on journeys from one city to another in the same country. (4)

The true tourist of the eighteenth century was, of course, the Englishman: eighty thousand of them every year, according to Gibbon, though he said he disbelieved the figure. The French Revolution and the Napoleonic Wars put an end to their foreign jaunts for a time, but as soon as peace returned hordes of better-off English people picked up the guide books of the eighteenth century and set off to the Rhine and spas of Germany and, as fashion changed, to the mountains of Switzerland.

The age of steam brought mass transport on land and sea, creating the lower fares which encouraged more people to travel. The flood of travellers led to the creation of new organisations to minister to their needs and these in turn provided an avalanche of paper to cover every operation.

Among the most famous of these organisations was the company founded by Thomas Cook. He saw the opportunity to provide cheap tickets for working people and in a remarkably short time had developed from a small-town excursion operator into the head of a huge international company.

Thomas Cook had been a printer in his youth and he had a natural flair for publicity, which he put to good use from the start of his career as an excursion agent by using printed paper to further his business. For his first trip in 1841, he printed a handbill which he personally posted on the walls of Leicester and the surrounding towns. From then on every excursion was advertised by handbills such as one printed in 1864 for an excursion to Leeds and Bradford. He also published a travel magazine (7) the cover of which, after he had established his world-wide tourist system in 1874, blossomed into colour.

As Thomas Cook's business grew, more and more hordes of tourists invaded Europe, becoming the butt of writers' and cartoonists' jokes. Songs were written about them. Typical was the *Cook's Excursion Galop*, making fun of their antics in climbing Mount Vesuvius.

The good-humoured jeers of such people as William Howard Russell and the English Consul at La Spezia were counterbalanced by the encouraging praise of town councils, hoteliers and proprietors of mountain railways who benefited from their presence. By the 1870s, when Thomas Cook was going round the world, the holiday industry in Europe was well under way.

For the collector, the field of holiday ephemera is varied, colourful, and in the period from 1880 to the present day, plentiful.

The resorts, vying with each other to attract customers, began early on to extol their own virtues and in the changing style of the leaflets and posters of over a hundred years, we may read a history of social manners and observances.

More than the resort, it was the hotel that was the main attraction and the style and quality of an establishment was a crucial factor in ensuring that customers returned year after year. In the early days, most of the regulars were recommended by friends and there was therefore little need for the hotel to do more than issue a simple pamphlet with a factual description of the amenities. However, by the turn of the century, the increase in numbers of people travelling, and therefore the potential

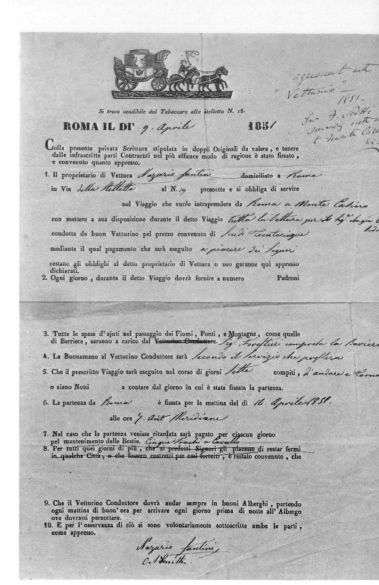

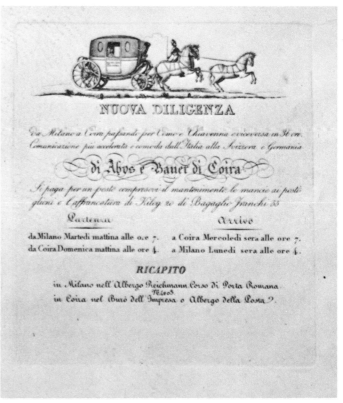

3. Travellers who could not afford private coaches took the 'diligenza' or public stage coach. These services were advertised by handbills posted at the places served. The Milan to Chur (Coira, in Switzerland), coach left Milan at 7.00 am. on Tuesday and arrived in Chur at 7.00 pm. on Wednesday.   153 × 133 mm

←1. The standard form of nineteenth-century contract for a horse coach could be bought at any tobacconist's. It included clauses about the feeding and overnight accommodation of coachmen. 368 × 255 mm

clientele, persuaded the hotels to draw attention to themselves more actively and hotel labels came into being; stuck on departing customers' cases they turned them into roving advertisements. Some of these labels, now rarely used by hotels, are most attractively designed and awake a nostalgia for a golden age of travel before travellers became packages.

Individuality, discretion and a homage to culture were the keynotes of those holidays and this is summed up in many of the brochures which, like the colourful Thomas Cook Holiday Tours brochure for 1909 (col. 13), stress the picturesque and historical aspects of popular tourist destinations, such as a castle looming over the Rhine and Mount Vesuvius outlined against a Neapolitan sky. The modern brochure in contrast leaves a very different message for the collector of the future. Here the glamour is more contrived and the promise contained in the illustrations is more Hollywoodesque in its treatment both of people and of hotels.

As hotels multiplied and their clientele grew, it became necessary to maintain a close control of bookings to ensure that those who had booked ahead were provided with the rooms they had ordered. It was in the hotelier's interest to encourage forward booking, for by this means he was able to forecast the results of his season. The hotelier was aided in this regard by the travel agent.

The success of Thomas Cook in helping hotel proprietors to fill their establishments, earned him the repu-

tation of having put the Swiss travel industry on its feet. One of the innovations which he introduced was the hotel coupon (9), an item which may be overlooked by collectors of holiday ephemera. The hotel coupon was carried by travellers, who handed it in to their hotel as proof of their booking. The coupon was valid for a range of prices and included a section for plain breakfast, another for dinner and a third for 'Bed, Lights and Attendance'. Gratuities were not included, but at least there was no VAT to pay. . .

At the turn of the century, the development of the hotel business was at its height in Europe and growing all over the world, particularly in those regions where the British sun never set. There is thus a vast potential store of ephemera related to it; hotel bills, restaurant bills, room notices, invoices from hotel suppliers and other revealing items. The differing life styles of the period divined at once by the items detailed; in some we find a frugality that suggests that the customer was one of the tourists whose visit abroad was a hard-won pilgrimage in the name of culture; others paint a picture of those robust Victorian men whose tastes for Limburger cheese and powerful cigars were no doubt responsible for the vapours from which Victorian and Edwardian ladies suffered.

2. Passengers' names and details of their excess luggage were entered on a waybill. This one was for a trip from Boston to Keene, which took thirteen hours and started at 5 am. 223 × 365 mm

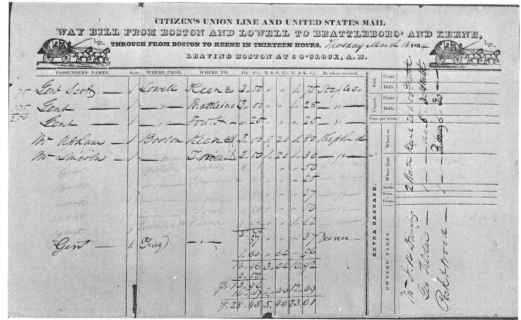

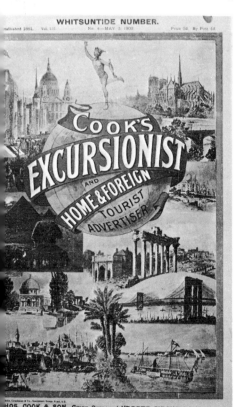

←7. In the early days of leisure travel it was usual to find a moral justification for taking a holiday. Health was a valid excuse for a seaside holiday and visits to cities were made for cultural reasons. The 1851 Great Exhibition in London's Hyde Park was the great cultural event of its time and Thomas Cook launched a magazine simply to persuade the workers to visit it. *The Excursionist* continued to be published until 1903 and then became the *Travellers Gazette*. 365 × 243 mm

Having settled down at the hotel, the tourist, then as now, looked around for ways to pass his stay pleasantly. Usually he was not disappointed, for wherever there is a tourist resort, there are people with an eye to persuading the visitor to part with his money. Among the chief occupations in the past was the daily excursion: the early trips by horse-drawn coach, later ones by motor chara-banc. In some parts of the world these forms of locomotion were replaced by others more exotic. In India it was common to see the sights from the back of an elephant and an excursion ticket issued in China, for a trip to the Ming tombs, orders the Railway Hotel, Nankow to provide the bearer with one Sedan chair and four coolies (11). Where railways had been established, excursions were often made by train, as in the Royal Kingdom of Siam, where travellers received coupons for 'Tiffin'.

As tourism grew, the forms of excursion became numberless. Every resort offered either conventional coach tours or some original form of transport of its own in which the tourist could explore the surroundings. Local electric trains and tramways built in the early days of electric traction exerted (and still exert) an inescapable charm on the contemporary tourist and they also provide him with agreeable items for his store of ephemera. The Manx Electric Railway provided passengers with an attractive view of the island on its leaflets and in Los Angeles the holiday visitor was offered a trip on a trolley car through the orange groves of California. Today the pleasure trips are often linked to means of transport developed by modern technology, or more violently with dizzy rides on cars that loop the loop, or the variety of excitements provided by Disneyland.

In Europe, many holiday pleasures remain traditional; providing its own modest excitement is the

4. Health certificates were required when travelling in certain areas in Europe. Venice was a notoriously unhealthy place, and this certificate, assures all whom it may concern that not only are specified passengers healthy but that the city itself is, too.
410 × 302 mm

8. Many people made fun of early travellers, especially those who ventured abroad. The popular excursion to Mount Vesuvius in Naples was the subject of this comic song about tourists.
347 × 252 mm

ferry-boat ride; the old chain-driven ferry at Bodinnick in Cornwall is typical. Tickets issued for trips such as these are ordinary indeed, but however humble, they tell a story and add to the recollected image of time and place.

Of all holiday ephemera, the item with the greatest appeal is of course the picture postcard. The habit of sending postcards began in the 1870s when resorts were becoming so crowded with 'trippers' that the former habitués began to go abroad to avoid the common throng. Whether one was at home or abroad, however, made no real difference as far as sending postcards was concerned.

In either case the motive was to let everyone know that one was on holiday, a message prompted to some extent by snobbery. The early cards were simply photographs of the resort and those sent from abroad continue to be of this kind to this day. Those from the English seaside, however, developed a form of comic commentary on the seaside scene (15). Demand was such that it became a profitable line of endeavour for professional artists, among whom the immortal name of Donald McGill ranks highest.

For the collector, the messages written on the back of the cards (after this was permitted by the Post Office in 1902), enhances their value. Those sent during the years of World War I are particularly poignant.

In the Edwardian period, the postcard indicated the change that was taking place in society, and pictures of couples embracing became popular while captions often suggested that the sender was enjoying a similar escapade (14).

In addition to the printed postcard, turn-of-the-century seaside visitors often posted photographs of themselves on the beach. These were taken by itinerant photographers who competed on the beaches with other roving salesmen. Despite the millions that must have been taken, these are a rare item for the modern collector.

Equally rare, and aesthetically one of the most delightful items of holiday ephemera, are song sheets depicting scenes from seaside, lake and mountain. Though some of these are also comic, making fun of the tourists and their antics, the majority are sentimental in character and express a nostalgia for holiday places that has helped the travel industry grow to its present dimensions.

In more recent times the production of printed matter relating to holidays has greatly increased the opportunities for ephemera collectors who want to specialise in this agreeable field. Today's collector will contribute to the historian of tomorrow a rich and varied picture of a revolution in social habits unparalleled in the history of the world.

9. The hotel coupon eliminated the need to carry large amounts of money by permitting travellers to buy coupons for meals and room before setting off on their journey.
120 × 80 mm

10. The Royal State Railways of Siam accepted coupons in payment for meals—including Tiffin.
110 × 185 mm

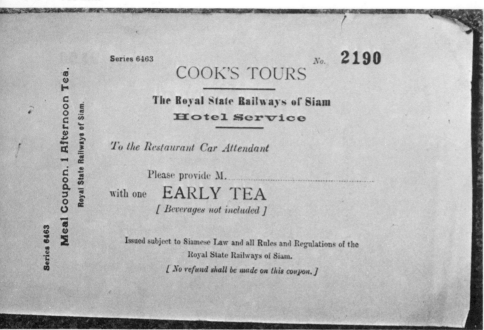

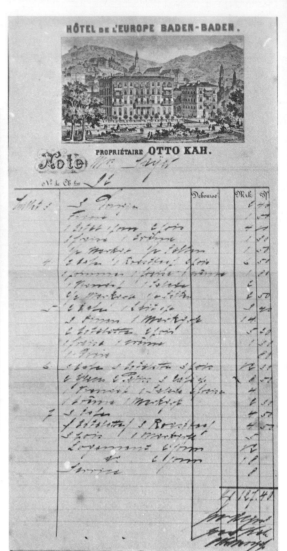

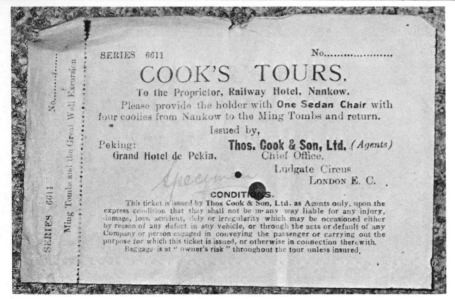

11. The coupon was a boon to travellers as almost everything on a journey could be paid for with it. This one covers the cost of a sedan chair with four coolies from Nankow to the Ming tombs and back.
100 × 155 mm

12. (Top) Hotel bills reveal details of holidays of long ago and they often carry attractive engravings of the hotels that issued them.
336 × 170 mm
(Above) Hotel room card. (Left) Guest list for Nile steamer which provided hotel facilities. 107 × 70 mm

6. Excursion agents and railway companies sought to persuade large companies to allow their employees to travel together and offered special low-cost arrangements for groups. This booklet was prepared for a Lever Brothers employee excursion to the 1900 Brussels Exhibition.
125 × 80 mm

15. Conditions at seaside hotels and boarding houses left a lot to be desired. They were the comic subject of many seaside postcards.
140 × 90 mm

My word if you're not off.

'It's simply glorious here!'

14. The habit of sending postcards began toward the end of the nineteenth century. These often had a romantic theme and suggested that life at the seaside was less inhibited than life at home.   90 × 140 mm

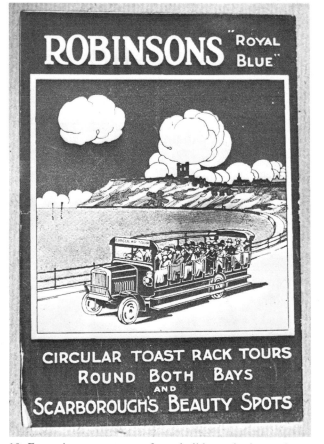

13. Excursions are a part of any holiday, whether at home or abroad, and the charabanc, now called a coach, has always been the principal vehicle tourists take to see local sights. The configuration of seats on this one, in rows open at each end, earned it the name of 'toast rack'.
179 × 120 mm

93

The history of transport and travel has been written up in so many books, including literally hundreds on the various individual themes of the subject, that it must be left to the reader to discover for himself those which meet his requirements. One book about transport in Britain which covers every aspect dealt with in this book, and which should alert the ephemera collector to many avenues worth exploring, is *The Transport Revolution from 1770* by Philip S. Bagwell (Batsford, London, 1974).

As for the subject of ephemera itself, two books are essential reading:

Collecting Printed Ephemera by John Lewis. Studio Vista, London, 1976.

Printed Ephemera by John Lewis. W S Cowell, Ipswich, 1962.

Other books which potential ephemerists will find invaluable are:

Label Design: the evolution, design and function of labels from the earliest times to the present day by Claude Humbert. Thames and Hudson, London, 1972.

The Picture Postcard and its Origins by Frank Staff. Lutterworth Press, London, 1966.

Printing 1770–1970 by Michael Twyman. Eyre and Spottiswoode, London, 1970.

The Public Notice: an Illustrated History by Maurice Rickards. David and Charles, Newton Abbot, 1973.

Saturday Book No. 20 ed. John Hadfield. 'A Golden Age of Advertising' by John Pitt. Hutchinson, London, 1960.

This is Ephemera by Maurice Rickards. David and Charles, Newton Abbot, 1977.

Victorian Delights by Robert Wood. Evans Brothers, London, 1970.

Among books more specifically about the ephemera of transport and travel, or which contain good ephemera illustrations, are:

King of the Road: an Illustrated History of Cycling by Andrew Ritchie. Wildwood House, London, 1975.

Picture Postcards and Travel by Frank Staff. Lutterworth Press, London, 1979.

Railway Antiques by James Mackay. Ward Lock Limited, London, 1978.

Railway Relics and Regalia gen. ed. P. B. Whitehouse. Country Life Books, London, 1975.

Roads before the Railways 1700–1851 by J. M. Thomas. Evans Brothers, London, 1970.

The Romantic Journey: the Story of Thomas Cook and Victorian Travel by Edmund Swinglehurst. Pica Editions, London, 1974.

16. The better-off holiday traveller tried to escape from the vulgar throng by going abroad. A few adventurous spirits travelled wherever there was a means of transport to take them. The Trans-Siberian Railway was the ultimate in railway travel, and still is. These tickets were issued for a journey from Hong Kong to Warsaw in 1912.
Cook's Ticket Cover 125 × 93 mm
Russian Cover 130 × 85 mm
South Manchurian railway 175 × 124 mm
Cook's itinerary 260 × 199 mm
Wagons Lit coupon 260 × 180 mm
Coupon 126 × 78 mm

Index
Text and mono illustrations

Index

Colour illustrations